Html & CSS Programming

The Ultimate guide on How you can write Html and CSS in Under 10 Hours

By Ted Dawson

Table of Contents

Chapter 1:
Introduction to HTML

HTML is very easy scripting language which stands for Hyper Text Markup Language. It describes web pages and you can learn basic creation of web pages with the help of this tutorial. Hypertext is a simple text that works as a link and Markup language means way to code layout information of a web page. An HTML Document is a simple text file which is read by the browser to display the web page. The code in the text file represents text, images, layout and links for other pages. So basic designing of the web pages is written in a normal text file using HTML language.

Benefits of Learning HTML

There are many editors in the market which creates web pages without any knowledge of HTML or CSS. You just need to take care of the layout and your web page is ready. However, if you want to be a good web designer learning and understanding HTML is very beneficial. You can learn from other web pages by reading the html code. You can use your own HTML tags to design the page or you can enhance the page with cool new effects which editor cannot do.

You can write the HTML code in simple text editor like Notepad which comes with Windows. Write the code in notepad file and save it using .html or .htm extension. Your web page is ready. Simple! Isn't it? Reading and writing the HTML code is also very simple. Just follow this guide and explore the world of HTML.

Working of the Web

Before we start with learning HTML code we should also know how web works. It will help you in web designing.

Computers who seek web/internet services are called as clients and computers who provide the internet services are called as servers. Servers store web pages, sites or apps. When client seeks a certain webpage, the server sends the data on to the client machine. The web page is downloaded on the machine to be displayed on the machine browser.

When you look at the website, it is most likely that you are viewing the HTML and CSS code that is coming from the server. Your browser converts the code into displayed format that you see. Most pages also contain JavaScript and Flash to your browser. These are advanced concepts. Once you learn the basic HTML and

CSS you can go for learning these advanced topics if you want to.

Most web pages also contain audio, video, images or animations. You will also learn how to incorporate these into your web pages.

Chapter 2:
Structure

After getting introduced to HTML we will start with the basic structure of HTML file. Any web page has got its own structure. Let's understand what structure is..

If you read any newspaper, then what you see in bold letters to catch your attention is a headline which you call as heading. The write up may be divided into several parts and each part can have subheadings- litter smaller than main heading. The article may have several paragraphs. And it may have some images to look more attractive or to give additional information. The structure of a web page (an online form) is very similar to the structure of a newspaper described above (offline form). You can see all the information of a web page described under headings, subheadings, paragraphs, images etc. This structure helps the reader to understand the content written on the page. So while writing the web page you should think about its structure first. If you are regular use of Microsoft Word, you will understand these terminologies quickly.

HTML Example

```
<!DOCTYPE html>
<html>
<head>
<title>Title</title>
</head>
<body>
<h1>Heading1</h1>
<p>paragraph1</p>
<p>paragraph2</p>
</body>
</html>
```

All normal web pages consists of two parts i.e. **head** and **body**.

Head

Body

The head part is not shown on the web page while the body part text is shown on the web page directly.

HTML Tags

HTML tags are the markups surrounded by open (<) and closed (>) angled brackets.

<tagname> Data </tagname>

The HTML tags usually come with pairs like <h1> and </h1>. The first tag is called as start tag while the second one is called as end tag. The end tag has a slash (/) before the tag name.

In the example above, the start and end of the document is depicted by <html> tag. <head> tag provides additional information about the document. <title> shows the title which is loaded at the top of the browser when the web page is loaded. <body> shows visible page content on the page.<h1> is the heading and <p> describes the paragraph on the webpage.

HTML Documents

To display the web page the <!DOCTYPE> declaration is required. There are various document types which are available on the web.

To display a document correctly, the browser must know both type and version. This declaration is non case-sensitive.

Web Page Creation

HTL web page can be designed using professional editors like Microsoft WebMatrix, Sublime Text etc. However for learning HTML you can use simple text editors like Notepad in Microsoft Windows or TextEdit in MAC.

You can follow below steps to create a web page using Notepad.

Step 1: Open Notepad in Microsoft Windows. (Click Run and type Notepad. Press Enter).

Step 2: Write or copy some HTML text in the notepad.

E.g.

```
<!DOCTYPE html>
<html>
<body>

<h1>HEADING 1</h1>
<p>This is a first paragraph.</p>
```

```
</body>
</html>
```

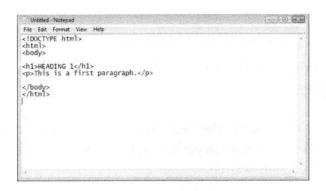

Step 3: Save the HTML page. Click on File->Save As. Give the file name with extension .htm or .html. Here we have given the name Example.htm. UTF-8 is the preferred encoding for these type of files.

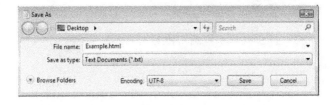

Step 4: Open the file in the browser. The result will be shown as follows.

Looking at Source code of a web page

Right click on the web page in the browser to look at the source code. Click on View Source or View page Source.

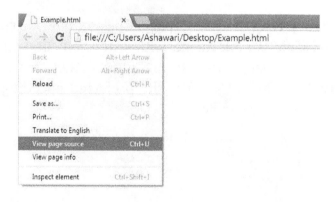

The source HTML code will be displayed in the browser.

```
1  <!DOCTYPE html>
2  <html>
3  <body>
4
5  <h1>HEADING 1</h1>
6  <p>This is a first paragraph.</p>
7
8  </body>
9  </html>
10
```

This is quite useful when you want to study new features available on a certain web page.

HTML Elements

The HTML element consists of start tag, end tag and data which is in between the tags.

For e.g.

<tagname> DATA </tagname>

Above entire statement makes an HTML element. Thus HTML element is everything starting from the opening tag to closing tag. Example given below:

<h1>Heading1</h1>

Nested HTML elements

All the HML documents consists of nested HTML elements

For example, below code have four nested elements.

```
<!DOCTYPE html>
<html>
<body>

<h1>HEADING 1</h1>
<p>This is a first paragraph.</p>

</body>
</html>
```

Empty HTML Elements

Empty HTML elements do not contain any data. For e.g.; **
** is an empty element which defines line break. An empty element can be closed in start tag like this:

HTML Attributes

HTML attributes gives additional important information about the content in the HTML element. They consist of two parts, name and value. An attribute is always placed in the start tag of an element. Name and value are separated by an equal sign. The attribute name indicates what kind of information about the element that attribute is going to provide. The value indicates the setting for the attribute. For e.g.;

<p lang="en-US">This is a first paragraph.</p>

Here, lang is an attribute name which provides the information about the language used to write the paragraph <p>. "en-US" is the value of the attribute which states the paragraph is going to be written in US English.The value is always written under double quotes.

We are going to look at different attributes used in the HTML coding as we progree in this tutorial.

Chapter 3:
Text

Entering text into the web page is very simple... Just add text into the code. If you do not specify any attribute, default font and size of the browser will be used. On the following pages you will learn how to customize the text settings on the web page. First we will talk about the headings and paragraphs and then formatting attributes of the text.

Headings

There are six types of heading used in HTML coding; i.e. <h1>, <h2>, <h3>, <h4>, <h5> and <h6>. Out of these, <h1> is used for main heading while <h2> is used for subheading. If there are further sections under sub headings you can use further heading levels. Browsers use different text sizes for different types of headings. The exact size of the headings varies with use of different browsers. User can also adjust the size of the text in the browser.

Using right type of Headings is most important. This is because the search engine makes use of headings to index the structure and content of your web page. Readers skim through the page looking at your headings. Caution is not to use headings for making text big or bold. Use headings for the heading purpose only.

Look at following example for knowing different types of headings.

```
<!DOCTYPE html>
<html>
<body>
<h1>This is main heading 1</h1>
<h2>This is subheading 2</h2>
<h3>This is subheading 3</h3>
<h4>This is subheading 4</h4>
<h5>This is subheading 5</h5>
<h6>This is subheading 6</h6>
</body>
</html>
```

You can check different heading sizes in the browser window.

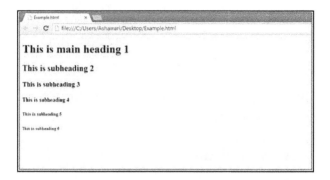

This is main heading 1

This is subheading 2

This is subheading 3

This is subheading 4

This is subheading 5

This is subheading 6

HTML Horizontal Rule

<hr/> adds horizontal rule in different sections of the web page. This an empty tag. To create between different themes this element is quite useful. You can see an example below.

<!DOCTYPE html>

<html>

<body>

<p>This is our first theme</p>

<hr/>

<p>This is our second theme</p>

</body>

</html>

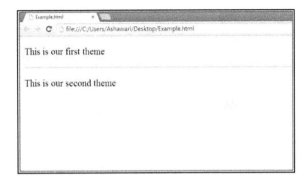

Paragraphs

The paragraph is shown with the help of the tag <p>. Between start <p> tag and end</p> tag, words of the paragraph are placed. By default, browser will place some space between two paragraphs. It will also start the new paragraph on new line. You can look at following example for details.

<!DOCTYPE html>

<html>

<body>

<p>This is our first paragraph.

The start of the paragraph is indicated by new line</p>

<p>This is our second paragraph. There is space between two paragraphs</p>

```
</body>
</html>
```

White Space

To enhance web page readability, authors may add extra space or strat text on new line. When the browser sees two or more spaces between two words it replaces that space with a single space. Even if the new content is on new line, it considers that space as a single space. This is called as '**white space collapsing**' .You can see this in below example.

```
<!DOCTYPE html>
<html>
<body>

<p>This is our first paragraph.</p>
<p>This is    our second paragraph.</p>
<p>This is
our third paragraph.</p>

</body>
</html>
```

Result:

Line Break

The browser automatically displays the new paragraph or new heading on a new line. However, to add a line break within a paragraph you can use the element <br/>. Please go through example below.

```
<!DOCTYPE html>
<html>
<body>
<p>This is <br/> our first paragraph where we are adding <br/> line breaks.</p>
</body>
</html>
```

HTML <pre> element

If you want to display preformatted text in the paragraph, you can use the element <pre>. The text inside the <pre> element displays both spaces and line breaks. So if you just replace the tag <p> with <pre>, you can display preformatted text.

HTML Formatting Elements

Special type of text can be display with formatting the elements. You can play with key words by making them bold,italics, underlined etc. It enhances the appearance of web page as well.

The key features provided by HTML are as follows.

- Bold text
- Important text
- Italic text
- Emphasized text
- Marked text
- Small text
- Deleted text
- Inserted text

- Subscripts
- Superscripts

Bold and Strong Formatting

You can make the character appear bold using the <b> tag without any extra importance. To define text with string sematic importance simply use the <strong> tag. Check out following example to understand these two terminologies.

```
<!DOCTYPE html>
<html>
<body>

<p>This is <b> bold </b> character.</p>
<p><strong> This is strong text</strong></p>

</body>
</html>
```

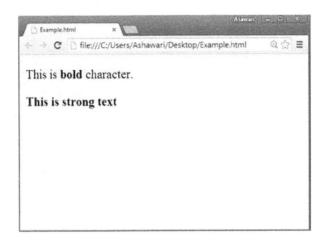

Italic and Emphasized Formatting

You can make the character look italic using the HTML tag <i> with no extra importance. You can emphasize the text with <em> tag with added semantic importance.

<!DOCTYPE html>
<html>
<body>

<p>This is <i>italics</i> character.</p>

<p><em> This is emphasized text</em></p>

</body>

</html>

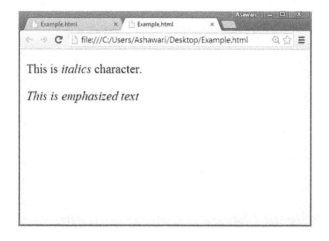

Bold and Strong text look the same in the browser. Similar is the case with italics and emphasized text. But there is a difference. Bold and Italics simply change the physical appearance of the text. However, strong and emphasized text makes the text 'important'.

HTML Small and Marked Formatting

<small> tag display the text as Small, while <mark> element highlights the text.

<!DOCTYPE html>
<html>
<body>

```html
<p>This is <small>small</small> world.</p>

<p><mark> This is highlighted
text</mark></p>

</body>
</html>
```

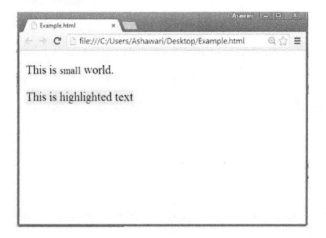

Deleted and Inserted Formatting

The HTML <del> element shows deleted or removed text, while <ins> element shows an inserted text.

```html
<!DOCTYPE html>
<html>
<body>
```

```
<p>This is <del>deleted</del> text.</p>
<p>This is
<ins>inserted</ins>text</mark></p>
</body>
</html>
```

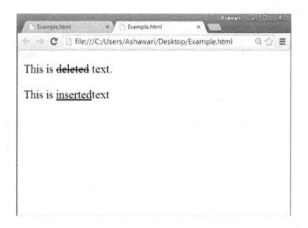

Subscript and Superscript Formatting

Making the text subscripted or superscripted is also very simle. Just use the tags<sub> and <sup> tags.

```
<!DOCTYPE html>
<html>
<body>
<p>This is <sub>subscript</sub> text.</p>
<p>This is <sup>superscript</sup> text.</p>
```

```
</body>
</html>
```

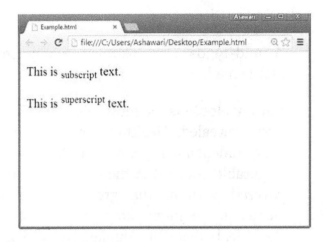

Quotations

Short quotation is represented by <q> element. Browsers insert quotation mark around the text surrounded by <q> element. When section has to be quoted, <blockquote> element is used. Browsers usually indent the part tagged by <blockquote> element. So, long quotations go with the element <blockquote>. Here is an example of both the elements.

Here is the quotation from Wikipedia as an example:

"I only hope that we never lose sight of one thing – that it was all started by a mouse."

—Walt Disney, Disneyland

A mid-1930s Nazi German newspaper article read:

Mickey Mouse is the most miserable ideal ever revealed...Healthy emotions tell every independent young man and every honorable youth that the dirty and filth-covered vermin, the greatest bacteria carrier in the animal kingdom, cannot be the ideal type of animal...Away with Jewish brutalization of the people! Down with Mickey Mouse! Wear the Swastika Cross!

<!DOCTYPE html>
<html>
<body>

<p>A mid-1930s Nazi German newspaper article read:</p>

<blockquote cite="https://en.wikipedia.org/wiki/Mickey_Mouse">

Mickey Mouse is the most miserable ideal ever revealed...Healthy emotions tell every independent young man and every honorable youth that the dirty and filth-covered vermin,

the greatest bacteria carrier in the animal kingdom, cannot be the ideal type of animal...

Away with Jewish brutalization of the people! Down with Mickey Mouse! Wear the Swastika Cross!

</blockquote>

<p>Walt Disney, Disneyland says:

<q>I only hope that we never lose sight of one thing – that it was all started by a mouse</q></p>

</body>
</html>

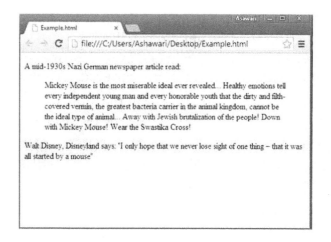

A mid-1930s Nazi German newspaper article read:

> Mickey Mouse is the most miserable ideal ever revealed... Healthy emotions tell every independent young man and every honorable youth that the dirty and filth-covered vermin, the greatest bacteria carrier in the animal kingdom, cannot be the ideal type of animal... Away with Jewish brutalization of the people! Down with Mickey Mouse! Wear the Swastika Cross!

Walt Disney, Disneyland says: "I only hope that we never lose sight of one thing – that it was all started by a mouse"

Abbreviations:

If you are using any abbreviation in your text, then <abbr> element can be used. It is used with the title attribute in the opening tag. Abbrevations provide more information to the transaltion systems,search engines and browsers. So make it a habit to mark the abbreviations in the text with <abbr> element.

<!DOCTYPE html>

<html>

<body>

<p><abbr title="The National Aeronautics and Space Administration"> NASA </abbr>

is the United States government agency responsible

for the civilian space program as well as aeronautics and aerospace research</p>

</body>

</html>

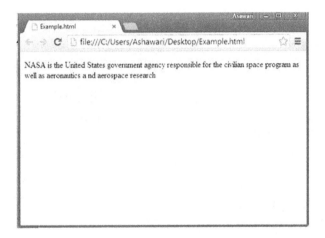

Citations and Definitions

The title of the work is defined by **<cite>** element. Browsers usually display <cite> elements in italic When you are referencing any article or research paper, <cite> element can be used to indicate the citations.

While defining a new terminology or introducing new concept, <def> element can be used. So show the defining instance with <def> tag.

```
<!DOCTYPE html>
<html>
<body>


<p><cite>The Da Vinci Code</cite> is a 2003 mystery-detective novel by Dan Brown</p>


<p> An <def>Illusion</def> is a distortion of the senses, revealing how the brain normally organizes and interprets sensory stimulation</p>


</body>
</html>
```

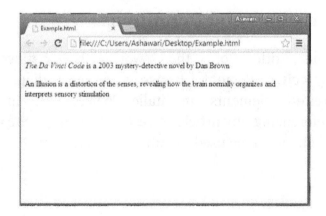

Address

Contact information of the author or the owner of a document or article can be shown by <address> element. The <address> element is usually shown in italic. Most browsers will add a line break before and after the element.

```
<!DOCTYPE html>
<html>
<body>

<address>
HAUZ KHAS <br/>
OH-2, Hauz Khas Village, <br/>
New Delhi - 110016 <br/>
Ph. 011-46054885

<address>
</body>
</html>
```

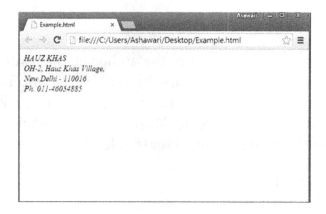

HAUZ KHAS
OH-2, Hauz Khas Village,
New Delhi - 110016
Ph. 011-46054885

Chapter 4:
Lists and Links

Lists

First we will look at Lists part of HTML. We use lists when we want to jot down the points together. The lists can be of three types; ordered, unordered or definition lists.

Ordered Lists: Each item in this list begins with a number. For e.g;

1. Number one
2. Number two
3. Number three
4. Number four

These items can be numbered with numbers as in above case or they can be numbered with alphabets (a, b, c or A, B, C) or roman numbers (I, ii, iii or I, II, III) etc.

Unordered Lists: Each item in this list begins with a bullet point. For e.g;

- Number one
- Number two

- Number three

- Number four

The items in this list don't have order. They can come in any sequence. Various types of bullets are available with HTML which can be used to design the lists.

Definition Lists: These lists are made up of set of terms along the definition of those terms.

Ordered Lists

The ordered list can be created using <ol> element. Each item in the list is enclosed by <li> element. By default, the browser indents the list.

Sometimes style attribute is used to set the type of the order (numbers, alphabets, roman numbers etc.). But it is much better to use the CSS list style property for that purpose.We will cover this part in CSS section.

Unordered Lists

The ordered list can be created using <ul> element. Each item in the list is enclosed by <li> element. 'li' means list item. By default, the browser indents the list.

Sometimes style attribute is used to set the type of the order (circles, squares etc.). But it is much better to use the CSS list style property for that purpose. We will cover this part in CSS section.

```
<!DOCTYPE html>
<html>
<body>

<p>Ordered List</p>
<ol>
<li> Number One </li>
<li> Number Two </li>
<li> Number Three </li>
<li> Number Four </li>
</ol>

<p>Unordered List</p>
<ul>
<li> red </li>
<li> blue </li>
<li> white </li>
<li> black </li>
</ul>
```

```
</body>
</html>
```

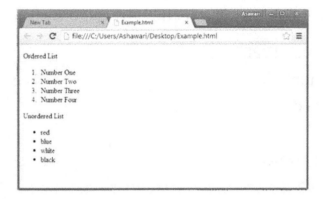

Definition Lists

The definition list is created using the <dl> element and it usually consists of series of definitions and terms.

Inside the <dl> element, <dt> and <dd> terms are used as pairs. <dt> is the definition term and <dd> is used to describe the definition term.

```
<!DOCTYPE html>
<html>
<body>

<dl>
  <dt>HTML</dt>
```

```
<dd>- HyperText MarkUp Language</dd>
<dt>CSS</dt>
<dd>- Cascading Style Sheets</dd>
</dl>

</body>
</html>
```

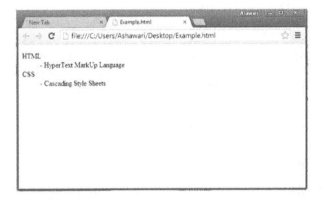

Nested Lists

To create a nested list, just put another list inside
<li> element. Browsers put an indent in front of
nested list further than the present list. If an
unordered nested list is created,browser put a
different type of bullet for the sub list.

```
<!DOCTYPE html>
<html>
```

```html
<body>

<ul>
 <li>Idli</li>
 <li>Dosa
  <ul>
   <li>Masala Dosa</li>
   <li>Sada Dosa</li>
  </ul>
 </li>
 <li>Medu Vada</li>
</ul>

</body>
</html>
```

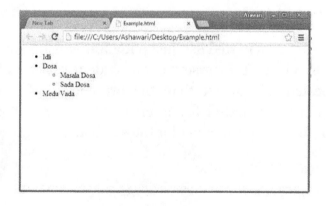

Links

Links are very important component of a web page as they are associated with the idea of web surfing or browsing. With HTML you can add a link to other web pages (external link) or link to a section of the same page (internal link) or links that open in new browser window.

The <a> Element

The anchor element <a> is used to create the link. Check out following syntax for more details.

<a href=https://www.gmail.com/> GMAIL</a>

The attribute 'href' states where the link should go and the text between start tag <a> and </a> (In this case GMAIL) becomes the shown hyperlink text (visible part). Clicking on the visible part will take you to the destination address.

The example above has absolute URL which takes you to the external link. Execute the above example on your PC. The visible text is shown with blue underlined text.(GMAIL). Click on the link and you will go to destination site in the same window.

Local Links

When you are linking to other pages on the same site, then you are creating local links. In case of local links, you only need to specify the file path. File paths for internal links can be absolute or relative. Absolute links always begin with a forward slash. They specify a path that starts at the root directory of your web server. Relative links never begin with a forward slash. They specify a path that is relative to the page that the link is on.

Examples of absolute links:

*   href="/"

: Go to the web root directory and get the default file. (The home page of the website)

• href="/ opportunities /

 : Go to the web root directory, then the opportunities directory, and get the default file.

• href="/opportunities/for-startups/startup-success-stories/writeup.html"

: Go to the web root directory, then the opportunities directory, then the for-startups directory, then the startup-success-stories directory, and get the file writeup.html

Examples of relative links

• href=" writeup.html "

: Get the writeup.html file that is in the current directory.

• href="../"

: Go up one directory from the current directory and get the default file.

• href="../../ for-startups /": Go up two directories from the current directory,

enter the for-startups directory, and get the default file.

As the examples demonstrate, URLs can vary in complexity while still pointing to the same location. For pages that are "near" the current page, relative links are often simpler. Relative links also work better if you are working with files on your desktop, as opposed to a real web server. Because absolute links are the same no matter where you are on the website, they're good for standard navigation links, header and footer links. However, absolute links don't work as well if you are just messing around with files on your desktop. On a web server, an absolute link such as / opportunities /writeup.html starts with the web server's root directory. But on your local desktop, there is no "web server root directory", and so your computer attempts to follow the file path / opportunities /writeup.html from the root directory of your hard drive. In general, this will fail.

The Target Attribute

The **target** attribute is used to specify how to open the hyperlink. There are various values of the attribute which you can use; for e.g. blank value means link will get opened in a new browser window. If the link is pointing to another website, then generally web page author wants the user to return to his website after finishing looking at other website. In such case, new window blank valued target attribute is generally used. Following is the syntax for the same.

<a href="https://www.gmail.com/" target="_blank"> GMAIL</a>

Other values for the target are as follows.

1. _self -> Open the link in the same frame (default)

2. _parent -> Open the link in the parent window

3. _blank-> Open the link in new window

4. _top->Open the link in the top window

5. _framename->Open the link in the named frame

You can try the example by replacing the value of target attribute.

Linking within Pages

Now we know how to create the external link or internal link. But what we want to create a link within the same page? In this case we create a bookmark which takes the reader to specific part of the same web page. This is particularly used if the page is long. In this case, first bookmark is created and then the link is added to that bookmark. The page will get automatically scrolled to the location specified in the bookmark.

Bookmark is created using following syntax:

<h2 id="bookmark">Bookmark added</h2>

Then link is added within the same page to go to the bookmark section.

<a href="#bookmark">Visit the bookmark Section</a>

Following example illustrate the linking in details.

```
<!DOCTYPE html>
<html>
<body>

<p><a href="#bookmark">Jump to Heading 4</a></p>

<h2>Heading 1</h2>
<p>This Heading something</p>
<h2>Heading 2</h2>
<p>This Heading explains something</p>
<h2>Heading 3</h2>
<p>This Heading explains something</p>

<h2 id="bookmark">Heading 4</h2>
<p>This Heading explains something</p>

<h2>Heading 5</h2>
<p>This Heading explains something</p>
<h2>Heading 6</h2>
<p>This Heading explains something</p>
<h2>Heading 7</h2>
```

```html
<p>This Heading explains something</p>
<h2>Heading 8</h2>
<p>This Heading explains something</p>
<h2>Heading 9</h2>
<p>This Heading explains something</p>
<h2>Heading 10</h2>
<p>This Heading explains something</p>
<h2>Heading 11</h2>
<p>This Heading explains something</p>
<h2>Heading 12</h2>
<p>This Heading explains something</p>
<h2>Heading 13</h2>
<p>This Heading explains something</p>
<h2>Heading 14</h2>
<p>This Heading explains something</p>

</body>
</html>
```

The result before clicking on the bookmark:

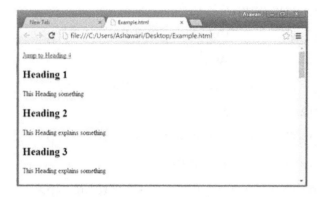

The result after clicking bookmark:

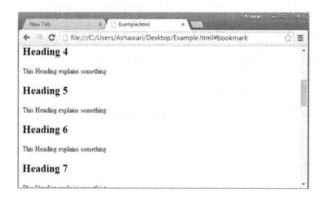

Chapter 5:
Tables

Tables are very useful to represent the data in grid format. The data is divided into rows and columns. It helps us to understand the data on two axes. Each block in the table is called as table cell. Let's take a look at how table is created in the HTML.

Table Creation

<table> element is used to create a table. The contents of the table are written out row by row. <tr> element is used to represent a start of each row. <tr> means table row. Each cell of the table is represented using a <td> element. A table row can also be divided into table headings with the <th> tag. Let's take a closer look at table creation with an example

```
<!DOCTYPE html>
<html>
<body>

<table>
  <tr>
```

```
    <td>A</td>
    <td>X</td>
    <td>1</td>
   </tr>
   <tr>
    <td>B</td>
    <td>Y</td>
    <td>2</td>
   </tr>
   <tr>
    <td>C</td>
    <td>Z</td>
    <td>3</td>
   </tr>
  </table>

 </body>
 </html>
```

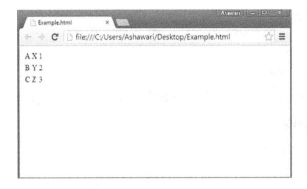

Table looks good with borders. We will learn how to draw borders around the tables using CSS.

Table Headings

The heading for either a row or column is represented using <th> element. <th> means table heading. Foe an empty cell you should use <td> or <th> element otherwise the table will not be created correctly. The scope attribute can be used on the <th> element to indicate whether it is row or column. It takes the values, row to indicate heading for a row or col to indicate heading for a column. The contents of <th> element is displayed in the bold and centered way. Table can also be given caption using <caption> tag.

<!DOCTYPE html>
<html>

```html
<body>

<table>
 <caption><b>Ticket Sales</b></caption>
 <tr>
  <th></th>
  <th scope="col">Saturday</th>
  <th scope="col">Sunday</th>
 </tr>
 <tr>
  <th scope="row">Tickets Sold</th>
  <td>50</td>
  <td>20</td>
 </tr>
 <tr>
  <th scope="row">Total Sale</th>
  <td>100</td>
  <td>150</td>
 </tr>

</body>
</html>
```

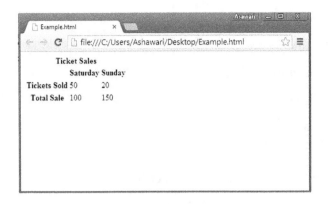

Spanning Columns

Sometimes you may need the entries in the table to stretch across many columns. For this purpose colspan attribute is used. It indicates how many columns cell should run across.

```
<!DOCTYPE html>
<html>
<head>
<style>
table, th, td {
    border: 1px solid black;
    border-collapse: collapse;
}
th, td {
    padding: 5px;
```

```
      text-align: left;
}
</style>
</head>
<body>

<h2>Cell that spans two columns:</h2>
<table style="width:100%">
 <tr>
  <th>Name</th>
  <th colspan="2">Telephone</th>
 </tr>
 <tr>
  <td>Mr ABC</td>
  <td>666 77 854</td>
  <td>888 77 855</td>
 </tr>
</table>
```

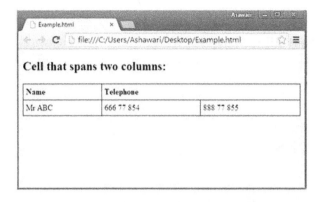

Note: I have used some CSS code for formatting table. You will learn more about it in CSS section of this tutorial.

Spanning Rows

To make a cell span more than one row, you can use the **rowspan** attribute. Check example below.

```
<html>
<head>
<style>
table, th, td {
   border: 1px solid black;
   border-collapse: collapse;
}
th, td {
```

```
      padding: 5px;
      text-align: left;
}
</style>
</head>
<body>

<h2>Cell that spans two rows:</h2>
<table style="width:100%">
  <tr>
    <th>Name:</th>
    <td>Mr XYZ</td>
  </tr>
  <tr>
    <th rowspan="2">Telephone:</th>
    <td>222 77 854</td>
  </tr>
  <tr>
    <td>888 77 855</td>
  </tr>
</table>
</body>
</html>
```

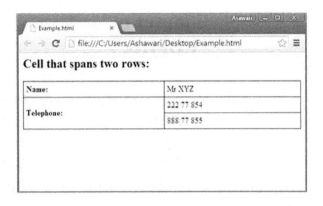

There is lot of code in HTML for formatting the table. But now we can use CSS for better formatting. Hence, details about table formatting in HTML have been omitted.

Chapter 6:
Forms

To collect different kinds of information from visitors of the site HTML Forms can be used. You will see forms for signing up for newsletters, signing up on the website, logging into account and shopping online. Right from adding simple search box on the site to creating more complicated applications, HTML Forms give you all kinds of flexibility to collect information from the user. There are various visible inputs of website like input text box, radio buttons, select buttons, password text box, list box, drop down box etc. We can create all with HTML forms. This lesson will teach you how to create forms for the website, different tools for collecting information and some advanced features with HTML 5.

The <form> element

All the form controls appear inside the <form> element. This element comes along with the 'action' attribute and usually has a 'method' and 'id' attribute too.

The Action Attribute

The action attribute defines the action to be performed when the form is submitted. The common way to submit a form to a server, is by using a submit button. Normally, the form is submitted to a web palop]

Nmnio,olo.

[p/ge on a web server. The value of the action attribute is the URL for the page on the server that will receive the information in the form when it is submitted.

The Method Attribute

There are two methods which you can use to send forms: Get or Post. You can use get (the default method) if the form submission is passive (like a search engine query), and without sensitive information. When you use get, the form data will be visible in the page address. The get method is ideal for short forms and when you are just retrieving data from the web server.

The post method is generally used in very long form. It is used when users need to upload file and or form contain sensitive data like passwords. When there is addition or deletion of data from the database, post method is useful. If the method attribute is not used, the form data will be sent using the get method.

The Id Attribute

Value of the id attribute is used to identify the form distinctly from other elements on the page. We will look at id attribute in details later.

The <input> element

The <input> element is used to create number of form controls. The value of the 'type' attribute determines what kind of input they will be creating

Type = 'text'

To create single line text input, the type attribute's value is 'text'.

The Name Attribute

Form controls are labeled using the name attribute. Web server should know data was entered into which control. To segregate information from different controls, naming the controls is a must. Identification of the form controls is done using the value of the name attribute. For example in the login form, server needs o know what data has been entered as username and data entered as password.

The maxlength attribute

The number of characters user can enter into text field is limited by the maxlength attribute. Its value is the number of characters they may enter. For example; a text that has to be entered is a year, the maxlength value needs to be four.

The size attribute

He size attribute should not be used on new forms. It was used in older forms to indicate the width of the text input. For example, a value of four would create a text box wide enough to display three characters.

In new forms CSS can be used to control the width of the text box. We will see this in CSS section.

Type='password'

When a type attribute has a value of password it creates a text box that acts as a single line text input except the characters are blocked out. The sensitive data such as password is not shown to the outside world. If someone is looking over the user's shoulder, he cannot see the password data. This type can also carry the name, maxlength and size attribute just like the typr as 'text'.

Although the password is hidden on the screen, this does not mean that the data in a password control is sent securely to the server. You should never use these sensitive data such as credit card numbers. For full security, the server needs o be set up to communicate with users' browsers using Secure Socket Layer (SSL) which is beyond the scope of this book.

```
<!DOCTYPE html>
<html>
<body>
<form action="">
Username:<br>
<input type="text" name="userid"
maxlength="8">
<br>
Password:<br>
<input type="password" name="psw"
maxlength="8">
</form>
</body>
```

</html>

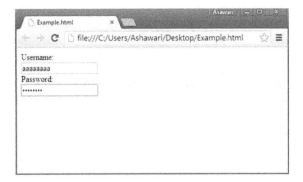

The <textarea> element

To create multiline text input the <textarea> element is used. This is not an empty element. Hence it should have a start tag and end tag. Any text that is written between start tag and end tag appears on the text box when the page is loaded.

If the user does not delete any text in the text box area, the same message will go to the server along with whatever the user has typed. CSS is used for determining the height and width of the text area. If you are seeing old code then you wil see the elements row and col used with this element.

<!DOCTYPE html>
<html>

```
<body>
<form action="">

Comments:<br>
<textarea name="comments"
cols="25"rows="8">
Enter your comments</textarea>

</form>
</body>
</html>
```

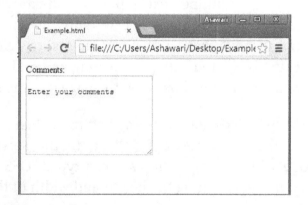

Radio Button Input

Radio button allows the user to pick one of the many options. <input type="radio"> describes the radio button. The name attribute is sent to the server with the value of the user selection. It distinguishes between different types of options. The value of the name attribute should be the same for all of the radio buttons used to answer that question. The value attribute indicates the value that is sent to the server for the selected option. The value of each of the buttons in a group should be different so that server knows which option the user has selected.

Checked

The checked attribute can be used to show which value should be selected when the page loads. The value of this attribute is checked. Only one radio button in a group should use this attribute. Once a radio button has been selected, it can only be deselected by clicking on another option.

```
<!DOCTYPE html>
<html>
<body>
<form action="">
  <input type="radio" name="sex" value="male" checked>Male
  <br>
  <input type="radio" name="sex" value="female">Female
</form>
```

```
</body>
</html>
```

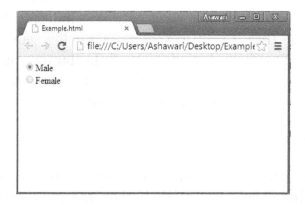

Check Box Input

Checkboxes allow users to select or unselect one or more options in answer to a question. The <input type = "checkbox"> is used to define the checkbox. The name attribute and the value attribute works similarly as the radio button. Also the default checkbox value is set by checked attribute value.

```
<!DOCTYPE html>
<html>
<body>
<form action="">
<input type="checkbox" name="car"
value="BMW" checked="checked">BMW<br>
```

```
<input type="checkbox" name="car"
value="AUDI">AUDI
```

```
</form>
```

```
</body>
```

```
</html>
```

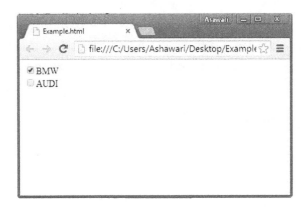

Drop Down List Box

A drop down list box allows users to select one option from a drop down list. The <select>element is used to create a drop down list box. It contains two or more <option> elements.

The <option> element is used to specify the options that the user can select from. The words between the start tag and end tag is shown to the user in the drop down list. The name, value and selected attribute work same as in the case of checkbox and radio buttons.

The function of the drop down list box is similar to that of the radio buttons. Key factors in choosing the right control out of the two:

If user needs to see all the options at a glance, radio buttons should be selected and if there is very long list of options drop down list box should be used.

```html
<!DOCTYPE html>
<html>
<body>
<form action="">
<select name="colors">
  <option value="red">RED</option>
  <option value="blue">BLUE</option>
  <option value="green" selected>GREEN</option>
  <option value="yellow">YELLOW</option>
</select>
</form>
</body>
</html>
```

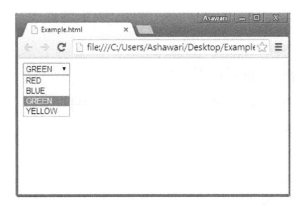

Submit Button

The submit button is used to send a form to the server. <input type="submit"> is used to show the submit button. The name attribute for this input is optional and you can give any name. However, it is better to provide value attribute as the words on the value attribute are displayed on the button. Otherwise the browser shows default value on the submit button.

Different browsers will show submit buttons in different ways. If you want to control how the button looks you can use CSS or you can use an image for the button. This part we will see later.

<!DOCTYPE html>

<html>

<body>

79

```
<form action="">
Subscribe<br>
<input type="text" name="email"/>
<input type="submit" name="subscribe"
value="Subscribe"/>
</form>
</body>
</html>
```

Label Controls

For labeling the controls <label> element is
used. Instead of using this element you can use
simple text. But especially for vision impaired
users the <label> element was introduced. This
element can be used in two ways. It can be
wrapped around both the text description and
the form input or it can be kept separate from

the form control and use the 'for' attribute to indicate which form control it is a label for.

The 'for' attribute states which form control the label belongs to. It is used in association with the 'id' attribute. The value of the 'for' attribute matches that of the id attribute on the form control it is labeling. This pair of 'for' and 'id' can be used on any form control.

The position of the label is very important while designing a form. There are some rules of thumb to place the labels on the form controls. For text inputs, text areas, select boxes and file upload labels are placed above or left to the controls. For individual check boxes and radio buttons, labels are kept to the right.

```
<!DOCTYPE html>
<html>
<body>
<form action="">
<label>Age: <input type="text"
name="age"/></label>
<br/>
<input id="indian" type="radio" name="citizen"
value="i">
<label for="indian">Indian</label>
```

```
<input id="foreigner" type="radio"
name="citizen" value="f">
```

```
<label for="foreigner">Foreigner</label>
```

```
</form>
```

```
</body>
```

```
</html>
```

Grouping Elements

You can group related form controls together inside the<fieldset> element. This is helpful for longer forms. Most browsers will show the fieldset with a line around the edge to show how they are related. The <legend> element can come directly after the fieldset start tag and gives the caption which helps identify the purpose behind grouping of controls.

```
<!DOCTYPE html>
<html>
<body>
<form action="">
 <fieldset>
  <legend>Contacts:</legend>
  Name: <br/> <input type="text"> <br/>
  Email: <br/> <input type="text"> <br/>
 Date of birth: <br/> <input type="text">
 </fieldset>
</form>
</body>
</html>
```

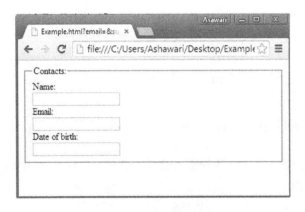

Chapter 7:
Images

To make a webpage attractive, you can add various kinds of images to it like photographs, logos, charts, and animated graphics etc. This lesson describes adding images to webpage using HTML, picking up right image format and showing image at right size. The formats which are used as images are .jpg, .png, .jpeg and .gif. Images which have few colors or large areas of the same color are stored in .gif or .png formats. When many different colors are present in an image it is stored as .jpeg.

Images are very important part of website. And pathway to a good website goes through adding great images. Images should be relevant and convey information. They should fit the color palette and should be instantly recognizable.

Adding Images

Images are added onto webpage using <img> element. It is an empty element and only consists of attributes. The first attribute is the 'src'. This is the location of the image file which browser searches for the image. This is usually a relative URL of the image. The second attribute is 'alt' which provides the text description. If a user cannot see the image due to certain reason, the alternate description of the image (alt attribute) is shown at the place of image. Thus alternative information is shown by the image. If the image is just to make a page look more attractive and it has no meaning, then the alt attribute should still be used but the quotes should be left empty.

You can also use the 'title' attribute for the image. This title is shown as a tooltip when you hover

```
<!DOCTYPE html>
<html>
<body>
<p>The alternate text shown when image not found:</p>
<img src="noimage.gif" alt="New Icon"
style="width:128px;height:128px;">
</body>
</html>
```

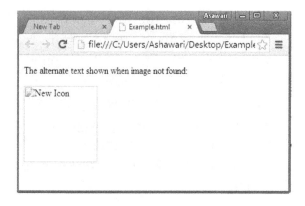

The animated images of .GIF standard are also accepted in HTML code. Using an animated image adds good visual appearance. Animated GIFs show several frames of an image ins equence and therefore can be used to create simple animations.

Image Size

There are two additionl attributes which are used to determine the size of the image.'height' attribute desscribes the height of the image in pixels whereas 'width' attribute describes the width of the image in pixels.

Images take longer to load than the HTML code of the rest of the page. Hence, it is agodd idea to specify the size of the image beforehand. In this case browser can render the rest of the text on the page while loading the image later on.

Size of the images nowadays is specified using CSS which we will se later on.

Storing Images

You can create a folder for all the images required for a web site. This will make the management of images easy. As the website grows, keeping images in separate folder helps to understand how the site is organized. All of the images are stored in a folder called 'images'. On a big website, usually subfolders are created within the images folder for better management.

Some websites store their images on image servers. In fact you can access the images from anywhere on the web by providing absolute URL.

Placement of images within the code

The images should be placed at the right place for better visual appearance. There are three ways to place an image. First is before a paragraph so that paragraph start on a new line after the image. Second is inside the start of a paragraph so that the first row of the text aligns with the bottom of the image. And the third way is to place the image in the middle of the paragragh.

Alignment of the images can be done using CSS code and that is better way. HTML5 does not support old alignment code of the images. Hence we will look at image alignment in the CSS section of this tutorial.

Image as a link

To use an image as a link, simply nest the <img> tag inside the <a> tag.

```
<!DOCTYPE html>
<html>
<body>
 Link for Google:<br/>
<a href="http://www.google.com">
 <img src="bird.JPG" alt="Search"
style="width:42px;height:42px;border:0;">
</a>
</body>
</html>
```

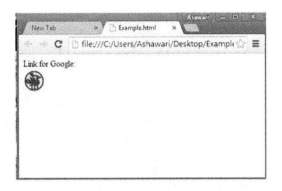

89

Chapter 8:
Extra Markup

In this chapter, we will learn some extra mark up tags used in the HTML like indicating version numbers of HTML, commenting the HTML code, using global attributes like class and id, embedding page within a page using iframes, adding information about the page etc.

Versions of HTML

There have been several versions of HTML and with each version HTML got evolved. The latest version which is in use is HTML5 which is widely used for creation of web pages. HTML5 was published in year 2000. In HTML5, web page authors do not need to close all tags, and new elements and attributes are introduced. So it is worth learning HTML5.

The <!DOCTYPE> declaration

There have been several versions of HTML. Each web page should begin with a DOCTYPE declaration to tell a browser which version of HTML the page is using.(Browsers usually display the page even if it is not included. However, to display the web page correctly

DOCTYPE should include both type and version. DOCTYPE is not case sensitive. All cases are acceptable. For e.g.

<!DOCTYPE html>

<!DOCTYPE HTML>

<!doctype html>

<!Doctype Html>

Common declarations of the versions are as follows.

HTML5

<!DOCTYPE html>

HTML 4.01

<!DOCTYPE HTML PUBLIC "-//W3C//DTD HTML 4.01 Transitional//EN" "http://www.w3.org/TR/html4/loose.dtd">

XHTML 1.0

<!DOCTYPE html PUBLIC "-//W3C//DTD XHTML 1.0 Transitional//EN" "http://www.w3.org/TR/xhtml1/DTD/xhtml1-transitional.dtd">

As you can see we have used HTML5 version throughout this tutorial.

Comments in HTML

For adding the comment to your code, you can add the text between these characters.

<!- -Insert comments here - ->

Comment will not be visible to the user's browser. Comment addition is very helpful because no matter how familiar you are with the page at the time of writing it, when you come back to it later, comment will make it more readable. Also if someone else wants to look at the code, comments will make it easier to understand. Although comments are not visible to users in the browser window, they can be viewed at the source code behind the web page.

On a long page you will often see comments used to indicate where sections of the page start or end, and to pass on notes to help anyone who is looking the code to understand it. Comments can also be used to block certain code so that it is not displayed on the web page.

Comments are also great for debugging HTML, because you can comment out HTML lines of code, one at a time, to search for errors:

```
<!-- Do not display this code at the moment
<a href="http://www.google.com">
-->
```

HTML comments tags can also be generated by various HTML software programs. For example <!--webbot bot--> tags wrapped inside HTML comments by FrontPage and Expression Web. As a rule, let these tags stay, to help support the software that created them.

ID Attribute

We have seen the ID attribute when looking at the web page forms. However, every HTML element can have ID attribute. It is used to give different identity from other elements. Its value should be a letter or an underscore. Number or any other character is not allowed as a value. No two elements should have the same value for their ID attribute otherwise the id will not be unique.

Giving an element unique identity helps to style it in better way with the help of CSS. This part we will see in the CSS section of this tutorial. If you are using JavaSript for web designing, id attribute can be used to allow the Java Script to work with that particular element.

As ID attribute can be used with any element, it is called as a 'global' attribute.

Class Attribute

Every HTML attribute can be accompanied by the Class attribute. It is generally used to identify several elements as being different from the other elements on the same page. For example, you might have some paragraphs of text that contain information that is more important than others and want to distinguish these elements. You may want to distinguish between internal and external linkages on the web page in that case marking with them with different classes will be useful.

Using these attributes does not affect the presentation of an element. It only changes the appearance if there is separate CSS rule being applied to them. If you would like to indicate that an element belongs to several classes, you can separate class names with a space.

Block Elements

Some elements will always get displayed on the new line in the browser elements. These elements are called as 'block elements'. Examples of block elements are <h1>,<p>,<ul>,<li> etc.

Inline elements

Some elemts will always continue on the sam eline as their neighbouring elemnts. These elements are called as 'inline elements'. Examples of inline elements are <img>,<b>,<em> etc.

The <div> element

To group a set of elements together in one block level box <div> element can be used. In a browser the contents of the <div> element will start on a new line, but other than this it will make no difference to the presentation of the page. With the help of id attribute and CSS you can change the representation of the elements grouped by <div>. The <div> element is very often used together with CSS, to layout a web page. Following the code becomes easy if <div> elements are used to hold each section of the web page. Such a way, several elements will be used in the web page. So, it will be helpful to add a comment at the end tag of </div>.

The <span> element

The <span> tag is used to group inline-elements in a document. The <span> tag provides no visual change by itself. The <span> tag provides a way to add a hook to a part of a text or a part of a document. The most common reason why people use <span> elements is so that they can control the appearance of the content of these elements using CSS. Usually class and id attributes are used with span element. This is to explain the purpose of span element and to apply CSS styles to elements that have specific values.

Iframes

To display a web page within a web page Iframes are used. Iframe is an abbreviation for the Inline Frames. You can see a small window like frame inside a webpage which is called as Iframe. Common usage os Iframe is to embed a Google Map into the web page.The syntax for Iframe is as below.

<iframe src="URL"></iframe>

Src attribute specifies the webpage which needs to be embedded. Apart from src there are some other attributes which are commonly used with the Iframes. The height and width attributes provide the height and width of the Iframe in pixels. There was a 'scrolling' attribute which was used in earlier versions of HTML. But it is not supported in HTML5. It is related to provision of scroll bar within a frame. 'frameborder' which is also an obsolete attribute in HTML5 is used for provision of border around the Iframe. 'seamless' is new attribute in HTML5 which depicts no provision of scrollbar. Older versions of HTML do not support this attribute.

```
<!DOCTYPE html>
<html>
<body>
<iframe src="Example.html" width="450" height="350"></iframe>
</body>
</html>
```

The <meta> element

Metadata is information about the data. The <meta> tag gives information about the HTML document. The Metadata will not be displayed on the web page. Meta elements are typically used to specify page description, keywords, author of the document, last modified and other metadata. The metadata can be used by browsers (how to display content or reload page), search engines (keywords), or other web services. The <meta> element is used with certain keywords to convey the information.

The most common attributes which are used with <meta> element are name and content attributes. These attributes are generally used together and they describe properties of the entire page. The value of the name attribute is the property you are setting and the value of the content attribute is the value that you want to give to given property.

The value of the name attribute can be anything you want it to be. Some defined HTML values are given below.

description

description of the page is given with this property. This description is used by the search engines to understand what the page is about. Maximum limit for this field is about 155 characters. It can also be displayed in search engine results.

keywords

keywords are used to find a page while using search engine. Hence comma separated keywords list is given by this field.

robots

This field indicates whether search engine should add this page into search results or not. A noindex value indicates that the page should not be added and nofollow can be used if search engines should add this page in their results but not any pages that it links to.

Like name-content pair,the <meta> element also uses http-equiv and content attributes. Some of the values of the http-equiv are as follows.

author

The author of the page is given in this field.

pragma

This prevents browsers from cachiing the page. Hence cache information is given in this field. Cache means locally saving the web page to save the time downloading it on the next visit.

expires

this option states when the page should expire. Please note the format of the expiry date in the examle shown.

```
<!DOCTYPE html>
<html>
<head>
<meta name="description" content="Web tutorials">
<meta name="keywords" content="HTML,CSS,Tutorial">
<meta name="robots" content="nofollow">
<meta http-equiv="author" content="Ms.ABC">
<meta http-equiv="pragma" content="no-cache">
<meta http-equiv="expires" content="Wed, 07 Oct 2015 23:59:59 GMT">
</head>
<body>
</body>
</html>
```

Chapter 9:
Audio and Video

You can embed music audio and video files onto your web page with the help of HTML tags. The new HTML elements like <audio> and <video> are used for this purpose. We will look at these elements in this chapter.

Audio

The <audio> tag is new to HTML, like the <video> tag, and allows developers to embed music on their websites (and unlike earlier attempts to add audio to a website, it isn't limited to old-fashioned midi music). That said, it does have limitations on the types of files that can be used. Currently any recent browser that is based on Webkit, such as Chrome and Safari, supports the use of regular .mp3 files. Others, such as Firefox, only support the .ogg format.

The good news is that you can either convert your files from .mp3 to .ogg (one audio conversion tool, media.io, can be used online) or just supply two versions of your audio file, one in each format. When Safari, for instance, comes across the <audio> tag, it will ignore the .mp3 file and move directly to the .ogg file.

Here is the audio tag in use (obviously you will only see it if your browser supports it):

You use the <audio> tag just like you use any other element:

```
<audio                          autoplay="autoplay"
controls="controls">
    <source src="music.ogg" />
    <source src="music.mp3" />
</audio>
```

You can also include the source file's location in the beginning <audio> tag, rather than between the two, like this:

```
<audio src="music.ogg" controls="controls">
```

Also note that you can point the src to a file located on the server with your web page (a relative URL, like /audio/music.ogg), or a file located elsewhere on the web (an absolute URL, such as http://www.yoursite.com/music.ogg).

You will likely want to include some text inside the tag so that users whose browsers do not support the <audio> tag will have a clue as to what is going on (and why they aren't seeing the audio control on the page). You do that like this:

<audio src="horse.ogg" controls="controls">

Your browser does not support the audio element.

</audio>

You can use any HTML elements that are supported within the <audio> tag, such as italics, bold, links, objects such as Flash, etc.

The <audio> tag supports the full range of standard attributes in HTML5. These attributes are supported by all HTML5 tags, with very few exceptions. They include:

accesskey - this specifies a keyboard shortcut for a given element

class - this specifies a class name for a given element, to be used in conjunction with a style sheet

contenteditable - specifies whether a user is allowed to edit the content

contextmenu - specifies the context menu for a given element

dir - specifies the direction of the text for content in a given element draggable - specifies if a user is allowed to drag a given element

dropzone - specifies the event that occurs when an item or data is dragged and dropped into a given element

hidden - specifies if a given element is hidden or not

id - specifies a unique identification for a given element

lang - specifies a language code for the content in a given element

spellcheck - specifies if a specific element will need to be subjected to a spelling and grammar check

style - defines an inline style for a specific element

tabindex - specifies the tab order of a specific element

title - specifies a title for a specific element

New attributes for the <audio> tag include the following:

autoplay - if this attribute is included, the audio will begin to play once it is ready

controls - if this one is included, controls for the audio file will be included on the page (which is a great idea--it is very annoying to not have a way to stop the audio from playing)

loop - if this one is included, the audio will loop and play again once it has finished

preload - this one has three parameters: auto, which plays once it has loaded,metadata, which only displays the data associated with the audio file, and none, which means it will not preload

src - this one's value is simply the URL of the audio file you wish to play

You can see some of the new attributes in action here:

```
<audio loop="loop" autoplay="autoplay"
controls="controls">
   <source src="music.ogg" />
   <source src="music.mp3" />
</audio>
```

The <audio> tag has a lot of attributes which can be used for additional controls, including the event attributes in HTML5. Events include window events, which are triggered for the window object, form events, which are triggered by actions that occur within an HTML form, keyboard and mouse events, and media events. Many of the events are the same as those included with previous versions of HTML. There are many new events for HTML5 though, and we will discuss them in an upcoming article on using events with HTML5.

Video

The HTML 5 <video> tag is used to specify video on an HTML document. For example, you could embed a music video on your web page for your visitors to listen to and watch. The HTML 5 <video> tag accepts attributes that specify how the video should be played. Attributes include preload, autoplay, loop and more. See below for a full list of supported attributes. Any content between the opening and closing <video> tags is fallback content. This content is displayed only by browsers that don't support the <video> tag.

The <video> tag was introduced in HTML 5 (officially referred to as HTML5 - without the space). HTML5 video is now widely implemented in the major browsers and it has support from major websites such as YouTube.

It works as follows.

```
<!DOCTYPE html>
<html>
<body>
<video width="320" height="240" controls>
  <source src="movie.mp4" type="video/mp4">
  <source src="movie.ogg" type="video/ogg">
  Your browser does not support the video tag.
</video>
</body>
```

The **controls** attribute adds video controls, like play, pause, and volume. It is a good idea to always include **width** and **height** attributes. If height and width are not set, the browser does not know the size of the video. The effect will be that the page will change (or flicker) while the video loads. Text between the <video> and </video> tags will only display in browsers that do not support the <video> element. Multiple **<source>** elements can link to different video files. The browser will use the first recognized format.

The full list of attributes for the HTML5 video element at this time includes the following, with usage notes:

- src - The URL of the video. This overrides the source element, if present.

- poster - The URL of a still picture to show while the video is not playing.

- preload - This can have the value none, metadata, or auto. Auto will download the entire file if possible; metadata will download just the parameters so that the length, size, and type of the video can be identified, and none will do nothing, which saves bandwidth.

- autoplay - This boolean, if present, triggers the video to play as soon as it is fully buffered or ready to stream.

- loop - Also a boolean; if loop is present, the video will repeat endlessly in the absence of user intervention.

- audio - This attribute, which controls the audio portion of the video, is still in development. Currently, it can take only a single value: muted, which means that the audio volume will initially be set to zero. The intent is to allow an autoplaying video to start and get the user's attention, but without blaring audio that would cause the user to close the entire tab in disgust :-)

- controls - A boolean attribute that specifies the browser should provide a set of default video controls. If it doesn't appear, you'll have to design and code your own controls.

- width, height - these size attributes control the size of the area reserved for the video on the page, but not necessarily its exact dimensions.

Chapter 10:
Introduction to CSS

Cascading Style Sheets (CSS) is used to handle the look and feel part of the web page. The representation of a web page depends upon the CSS. HTML handles the content part of the web page. Hence CSS is used along with HTML or XHTML to design the web pages. CSS can control multiple web pages all at once. A certain web page can be represented in several ways using CSS. It also saves a lot of work which earlier was done using HTML. It controls the style, layout and display of various sections of the web page. You can draw boxes around text and specify its border, height and width etc. You change background color as well. Changing the text appearance is also easy with CSS. You can change font, color and size of the text. Using CSS for web page designing is fun! There are various advantages of using CSS. They are as follows.

- First of all it saves time. The style definitions are generally saved in external .css files. Just by changing one file, you can change the look of an entire web site. Or you can use that file for designing many web pages.

- With CSS, the downloading of web pages onto the browser becomes faster. You need not write HTML attributes for all tags. Just set one CSS rule of a tag and apply it to all its occurrences. Easy! Less code automatically means faster downloading.

- Maintenance of websites becomes easy with the CSS files. To make a global change, simply change one file. All pages will be changed automatically.

- CSS can be used with multiple devices. Style sheets can be made compatible for different types of devices such as computers, cell phones and printers etc.

- There are global standards of CSS. Hence it is better to use CSS to design the web pages which are compatible with future browsers.

- It gives better look to HTML page. Styles look much elegant than just HTML page.

Earlier HTML was the only language used to design the web page. But it never intended to have formatting tags. The stress was given only on the content of the web page. When tags like

<font>, and color attributes were added to the HTML 3.2 specification, it started a nightmare for web developers. Development of large web sites, where fonts and color information were added to every single page, became a long and expensive process. To solve this problem, the World Wide Web Consortium (W3C) created CSS. CSS was created to specify the document's style, not its content. In HTML 4.0, and later, all formatting should be removed from the HTML page, and stored in separate CSS files.

CSS is very simple design language which is easy to understand. We will go through various aspects of designing web pages using CSS.

CSS Syntax

CSS consists of certain style rules which are interpreted by browsers and applied to certain elements of the web page. Each style rule contains a selector and declaration block. Syntax is as follows.

Selector {property:value;}

Selector is HTML element to which CSS rule is being applied. This could be any HTML tag. Within a declaration block {}, multiple pairs of property and value are given separated by semi colons. Property and value are separated by a colon. Property is any HTML attribute like color, fonts etc. Most of the HTML attributes are CSS properties. Values are assigned to each property as per web designer's preference. A CSS declaration ends with semicolon and declaration block surrounds with curly brackets as shown above. Example is here.

h1 {color:blue ;font-size:12px;}

Here, h1 is the selector. Color and font-size are the properties of h1. Their respective values are blue and 12px. Let's make a simple CSS style. We will make one centre aligned blue colored paragraph. CSS style is enclosed under <style> tag in html file.

```
<!DOCTYPE html>
<html>
<head>
<style>
p { color: blue;  text-align: center;}
</style>
</head>
<body>
<p> Welcome to the world of CSS!</p>
```

<p>We will make this paragraph blue colored and centre aligned. </p>

</body>

</html>

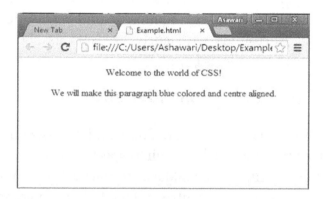

CSS Comments

Comments provide additional information about the code. These comments are ignored by the browsers and you can use these comments to edit code later if required. Comments are given within /* and */ syntax.

/*Write comment Here*/

CSS Selectors

HTML elements are selected and manipulated using CSS selectors. Style is provided tooth elements using these selectors. There are different kinds of selectors described below.

The element selector

Based on the element name, these types of selectors select elements. Same kind of selector is described above. One more example is given below for better understanding.

table{border :1px solid #C00;}

Table is given border of 1 pixel with black color. You will learn to work with different elements in coming chapters.

The id selector

The id selector uses the id attribute of elements to select particular element. The id should be unique to that particular page. Id selector is written with a hash element followed by name of the id. If you want to select single element the id attribute can be used.

#new_para { color: blue; text-align: center;}

Above style will be applied to an HTML element with id attribute set as new_para. We will take another specific example.

h2#RED{color:red}

Above selector will select all the h2 elements with an id attribute set as RED. And all these elements will be applied red color.

```
<!DOCTYPE html>
<html>
<head>
</head>
<body>
<style>
 h2#RED {color: red;}
</style>
</head>
<body>
<h1>HEADING1<h1>
<h2 id="RED">HEADING2<h2>
<h2>HEADING2<h2>
<h2 id="RED">HEADING2<h2>
</body>
</html>
```

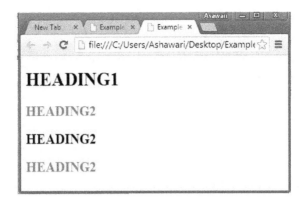

Note that only heading2, with RED id attribute are shown in read.

The Class Selector

A specific style rule can be applied to all the elements having a certain class attribute. It is defined by a period character followed by the name of the class attribute. In the example below, all the elements with internal class will have blue colored text.

.internal {color: blue;}

In the above cases all the elements in the internal class will be applied the style. To limit this only to particular elements, precede the period character with element name. For example,

h1.internal{color:blue}

Now only the h1 elements with internal class will have blue color.

```
<!DOCTYPE html>
<html>
<body>
<style>
h1.internal{color:blue}
</style>
</head>
<body>
<h1 class="internal">HEADING1<h1>
<h2>HEADING2<h2>
<h1>HEADING1<h1>
<h2 class="internal">HEADING2<h2>
<h1 class="internal">HEADING1<h1>
</body>
</html>
```

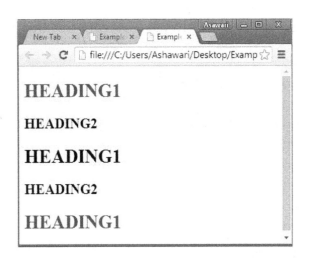

The descendent selector

This type of selector applies the style rule to the element only when that particular element is present inside another element. For example in the example below, 'b' element will get red color only when it is under ul element.

ul b {color : red}

The Universal selector

This type of selector applies the style rule to all the elements rather than specifying particular elements.

*{color:red}

Every element will have red color with this type of selector.

Grouping selectors

If you have number of selectors whose style rules are same. Then you can group those selectors. You can minimize the code by this method.

```
h1 {
    text-align: center;
    color: red;
}

h2 {
    text-align: center;
    color: red;
}

p {
    text-align: center;
    color: red;
}
```

Instead of this you can join them together like this:

```
h1, h2, p {
```

```
    text-align: center;

    color: red;

}
```

Individual elements are separated by comma. Similarly you can join different class selectors having same style rule.

```
#class1, #class2, #class3 {

    text-align: center;

    color: red;

}
```

CSS Attribute Selectors

HTML attributes are used to style the elements that have specific attribute values. We will see how the attribute values help in styling the web page.

[Attribute] selector

The [attribute] selector is used to style the element with a specified attribute given in the square brackets.

p[lang] {color: red} -> This example styles all 'p' elements with 'lang' attribute.

[Attribute=”value”] selector

The [Attribute=”value”] styles all the elements with a specified attribute-value pair.

p[lang=”eng”] {color:red} -> This example styles all the 'p' elements whose attribute lang has the exact value of "eng".

[Attribute~=”value”] selector

The [attribute~="value"] selector is used to select elements with an attribute value containing a specified word.

P[lang~=”eng”] -> This example styles all the elements having lang attribute with value containing the space separated list of words one of which is "eng". It can match elements with lang=”eng”, lang=”eng US”,lang=”eng India” but not lang=”eng-UK”

[Attribute|=”value”] selector

The [attribute~="value"] selector is used to select elements with an attribute starting with the specified value.

p[lang|=”eng”] -> This example styles all the elements having lang attribute with starting value exactly as 'eng' or begin with 'eng-'.

[Attribute^="value"] selector

The [attribute^="value"] selector is used to select elements with an attribute starting with the specified value.

p[lang^="eng"] -> This example styles all the elements having lang attribute with starting value 'eng' or begins with 'eng'. The value does not have to be whole word.

[Attribute$="value"] selector

The [attribute$="value"] selector is used to select elements with an attribute value ending with the specified value.

p[lang$="UK"] -> This example styles all the elements having lang attribute with the value that ends with 'US'. The value does not have to be whole word.

[Attribute*="value"] selector

The [attribute*="value"] selector is used to select elements with an attribute value that contains specified letters.

p[lang*="en"] -> This example styles all the elements having lang attribute with the value that contains letters 'en'. The value does not have to be whole word.

Ways to insert the CSS

There are following three ways to insert the style sheets.

- Internal Style Sheet
- External Style Sheet
- Inline style

Internal Style Sheet

You can insert the style rules inside the HTML page within the <style> element inside the head section. It is generally used if a single page has to be designed with unique style.

```
<!DOCTYPE html>
<html>
<head>
<style>
body {
   background-color: pink;
}
h1 {
   color: red;
```

```
    margin-left: 40px;
}
</style>
</head>
<body>
<h1>Heading</h1>
<p>This is a paragraph.</p>
</body>
</html>
```

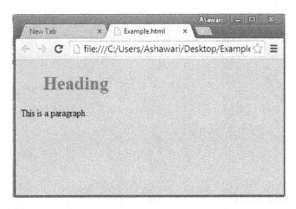

External Style Sheet

An external .css file can contain all the style rules needed for an entire web site. This file can be imported in the HTML file using <link> element. The <link> element comes under <head> section.

```
<head>
<link rel="stylesheet" type="text/css"
href="newstyle.css">
</head>
```

An external style sheet can be written in any text editor. The file should not contain any html tags. The style sheet file must be saved with a .css extension. An example of a style sheet file called "newstyle.css", is shown below:

```
body {
    background-color: pink;
}
h1 {
    color: red;
    margin-left: 40px;
}
```

Inline style

An inline style may be applied to a single element. This may lead to losing many advantages of a style sheet as content gets mixed with presentation. So advice is to use this method sparingly.

The style attribute is added to the relevant tag to make the CSS style inline. The attribute can have any CSS property. Following example shows the inline style of <h1> tag.

To use inline styles, add the style attribute to the relevant tag. The style attribute can contain any CSS property. The example shows how to change the color and the left margin of a <h1> element:

<h1 style="color:blue;margin-left:30px;">This is a heading.</h1>

Overriding Rule of Style Sheets

If there are multiple styles defined for HTML element, then there is an overriding rule which decides which one will be applied to the HTML element. Inline styles have higher priority above external style sheets and internal style sheets. So it will override the style inside <head> tag or style defined in external CSS file. Also internal style sheets have higher priority above external one. Hence, it will override the style defined in external file.

Chapter 11:
Color

It is good to understand how to apply various colors in the style rules. Mainly color values are required to specify a color. These values are used to specify either the foreground color or the background color of the elements. They add decorative effect to the elements as well. There are various ways in which color values can be described as shown below.

HEX Color codes

CSS supports six digit hexadecimal representations of colors. Out of the six digits, first two digits have (RR) red values. Middle two digits have (GG) green values and last two digits have (BB) blue values. This hexadecimal value can be taken from any graphics related software like Adobe Photoshop, advanced Paint Brush etc. Each hexadecimal value is preceded by hash sign. Following is the example of color and its hexadecimal representation.

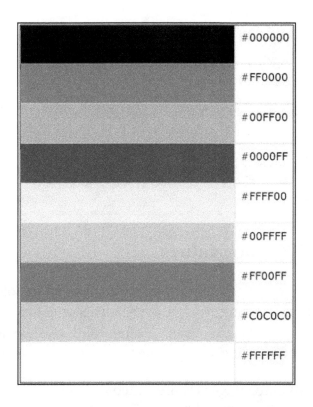

	#000000
	#FF0000
	#00FF00
	#0000FF
	#FFFF00
	#00FFFF
	#FF00FF
	#C0C0C0
	#FFFFFF

Short Hex Color Code

Shorter forms of hex color code are also supported in CSS. Three digit representation of hex color value preceded with hash sign is used. The value can be taken from Graphics software. Following is the example of short hex values.

	#000
	#F00
	#0F0
	#0FF
	#FF0
	#0FF
	#F0F
	#FFF

RGB Color values

RGB value consists of Red, Green and Blue Color values ranging from 0 to 255. This is called rgb property of the color. This RGB can be an integer or percentage value.

RGB percentage is represented as rgb(rrr%,ggg%,bbb%). For example, rgb(25%,50%,75%)

RGB absolute value is represented as rgb(rrr,ggg,bbb). For example, rgb(0,255,255).

Color	Color RGB
	rgb(0,0,0)
	rgb(255,0,0)
	rgb(0,255,0)
	rgb(0,0,255)
	rgb(255,255,0)
	rgb(0,255,255)

Color Names

There are different 147 color names which are predefined and are supported by browsers. So, absolute color names can also be used. For example, color:teal.

Chapter 12:
Text

Text is the important part of the web page. It can be formatted using certain CSS properties. The appearance of the text can be changed to suit the background. This chapter describes various text related properties.

Text Color

The color of the text can be changed by setting the color of the text elements.The default text color is set in the body selector.

```
<!DOCTYPE html>
<html>
<head>
<style>
body {
    color: pink;
}
h1 {
    color: blue;
}
p.class1 {
```

```
    color: rgb(0,255,255);
}
</style>
</head>
<body>
<h1>Heading 1-> Set to blue color</h1>
<p>The default color is set to pink as defined in
the body selector.</p>
<p class="class1">This is paragraph with rgb
value (0,255,255) </p>
</body>
</html>
```

Text Alignment

The horizontal alignment can be set using text-align property. Text can be right aligned,left aligned, centered aligned or justified. Justified alignment means lines are stretched to have equal width.

```
<!DOCTYPE html>
<html>
<head>
<style>
h1 {
    text-align: center;
}
p.date {
    text-align: right;
}
p.main {
    text-align: justify;
}
</style>
</head>
<body>

<h1>Text-alignment Centered</h1>
<p class="date">October, 2015</p>
```

```html
<p class="main">Images may be two-dimensional, such as a photograph, screen display,
```

```html
and as well as a three-dimensional, such as a statue or hologram. They may be captured by optical devices – such as cameras, mirrors, lenses, telescopes, microscopes, etc.
```

```html
and natural objects and phenomena, such as the human eye or water.</p>
```

```html
<p><b>Note:</b> Resize the browser window to see how the value "justify" works.</p>
```

```html
</body>
```

```html
</html>
```

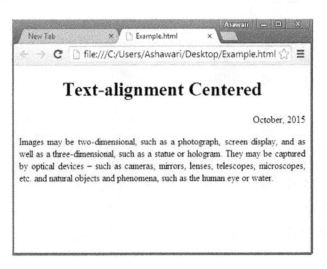

Text decoration

The text-decoration property can be used to set or remove the decoration from the text. The values which can be set are none, underline, line-through, overline etc. We will see each of the property in the following example.

```
<!DOCTYPE html>
<html>
<head>
<style>
h1 {
    text-decoration: overline;
}
h2 {
    text-decoration: line-through;
}

h3 {
    text-decoration: underline;
}
</style>
</head>
<body>
```

```
<h1>Heading 1</h1>
<h2>Heading 2</h2>
<h3>Heading 3</h3>
</body>
</html>
```

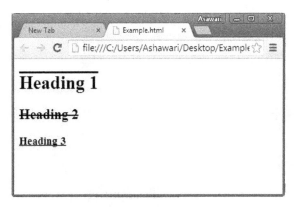

Text Transformation

The text-transform property can be used to change the letters of the text as lowercase or uppercase. It can also be used to capitalize the first letter of the word.

```
<!DOCTYPE html>
<html>
<head>
<style>
p.uppercase {
```

```
    text-transform: uppercase;
}
p.lowercase {
    text-transform: lowercase;
}

p.capitalize {
    text-transform: capitalize;
}
</style>
</head>
<body>
<p class="uppercase">This paragraph will be written in upercase</p>
<p class="lowercase">This paragraph will be written in lowercase.</p>
<p class="capitalize">This paragraph will be written with catialized letters.</p>
</body>
</html>
```

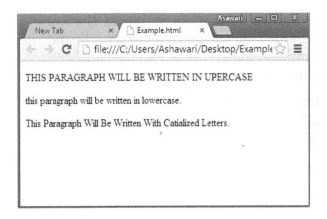

Text Indent

The text shadow property allows the first line to be indented by given value. This value can be given in pixels, or cms.

```
<!DOCTYPE html>
<html>
<head>
<style>
p {
    text-indent: 50px;
}
</style>
</head>
<body>
```

<p>Known throughout the world, the works of William Shakespeare have been performed in countless hamlets, villages, cities and metropolises for more than 400 years.

And yet, the personal history of William Shakespeare is somewhat a mystery.</p>

</body>   .

</html>

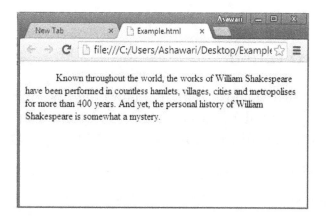

Spacing between Characters and Words

Adjusting space between words is called as Kerning. Typographers usually use this terminology. You can set the space between letters with the help of letter-spacing property. When your heading or sentence is in uppercase, it is useful to increase the kerning between letters. Otherwise in normal case when the text is in lowercase, increasing or decreasing kernel affects the readability of the text.

```
<!DOCTYPE html>
<html>
<head>
<style>
h1,h2 {
    text-transform: uppercase;
    letter-spacing: 10px
}
h1.normal {
    text-transform: uppercase;
    letter-spacing: normal
}
</style>
</head>
<body>
<h1> HEADING1 <h1>
<h2> HEADING2 <h2>
<h1 class="normal"> HEADING1 <h1>
</body>
</html>
```

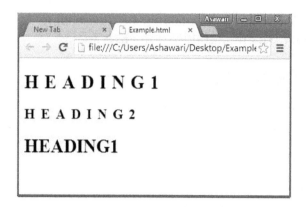

The spacing between words can also be set using the word-spacing property. You need not change this property regularly. If the typeface is bold or you have increased the letter spacing, in that case it would be better to increase word spacing. This will improve readability.

```
<!DOCTYPE html>
<html>
<head>
<style>
p {
    text-transform: uppercase;
    word-spacing: 10px
}
p.normal {
    text-transform: uppercase;
```

word-spacing: normal

}

</style>

</head>

<body>

<p> This is paragraph with word spacing set for 10px <p>

<p class="normal"> This is normal paragraph with normal word spacing <p>
</body>

</html>

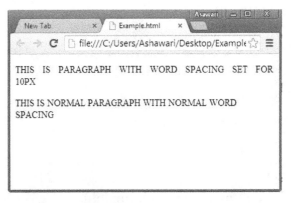

Text Shadow

To apply a shadow effect on the text text-shadow property is used. It creates the embossing effect to the letters. The shadow is dark version of the word just behind it and slightly offset. Setting the value of this property is slightly complicated. Three lengths and color of the shadow has to be entered. The first length indicates how far the shadow should reach to the right or left of the letter. The second length indicates the top or bottom distance that letter should cover. The third length is optional which states the amount of blur applied to shadow. The fourth value is the color of the shadow. This text-shadow property is supported by very few browsers. So check it before using it.

```
<!DOCTYPE html>
<html>
<head>
<style>
h1.red {
   text-shadow: 2px 2px 8px red;
}
h1.blue {
   text-shadow: -8px -8px 0px blue;
}
h1.green {
   text-shadow: 4px -4px 2px green;
}
</style>
```

```
</head>
<body>
<h1 class="red"> Heading 1 </p>
<h1 class="blue"> Heading 1 </p>
<h1 class="green"> Heading 1 </p>
</body>
</html>
```

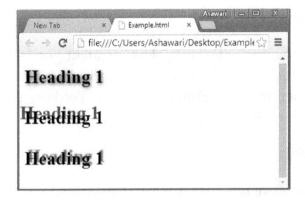

Text Fonts

Now we will look at how the fonts of the text are set with the help of CSS. It includes setting font properties such as font families, size, boldness and style. First we will understand font families.

Serif Fonts:

This type of fonts has small lines at the end of some characters. These small lines are called as

Serif strokes. Fonts like Times New Roman, Georgia come under this type. Serif fonts are easier to read and are used for writing long passages. Let's take a closer look at the Serif type

Times New Roman

You can see the smaller lines called Serifs at the end.

Sans Serif Fonts

This type of fonts has straight ends for characters. If the text is small the font is much easier to read. Fonts like Arial, Verdana come under this type. Let's take a closer look.

Arial

There are no serifs at the end of letters.

Monospace

This type of font family has letters with equal width. Monospace fonts are usually used for code because they align nicely. Fonts like Courier New, Lucida Console come under this type of font family.

Courier New

You can notice equal width letters.

It is important to understand that the browsers will display the chosen font of web page only if the font is installed on the user's computer.

Font Family

The font-family property allows setting the fonts for the text for various HTML elements. Series of fonts have to be specified for this property. If one font doesn't exist on the system, the browsers search for the next one. The last option sets the generic font family. The browser can choose the fonts from that family if the earlier options of fonts are not working. This is called fallback system of the fonts. So start with the font that you want to set and end with a generic font family. If the name of the font is more than one word then put the name in the quotation marks.

```
<!DOCTYPE html>
<html>
<head>
<style>
body {
    font-family: Georgia, Times, serif;
}
p.serif {
    font-family: "Times New Roman", Times, serif;
```

```
}
p.sansserif {
    font-family: Arial, Helvetica, sans-serif;
}
p.manospace {
    font-family: "Courier New", Courier,
monospace;
}
</style>
</head>
<body>

<h1>CSS font-family (Georgia font)</h1>
<p class="serif">This paragraph is in the Times
New Roman font.</p>
<p class="sansserif">This paragraph is in the
Arial font.</p>
<p class="monospace">This paragraph is in the
Courier New font.</p>
</body>
</html>
```

Font Style

Font style is used to specify the italic style of the fonts. It has three values :normal,italic and oblique. Normal value means the text will be shown without italics. To make the text italic, value is set as italic. To make the text oblique i.e. slightly tilted; set the value as oblique.

Italic fonts are stylized versions of the font based on calligraphy. And oblique version simply takes the normal version and put it at an angle. If browser does not find an italic version of a font, it uses an algorithm to place the normal font at an angle. So, lt of italic text online is actually oblique.

```
<!DOCTYPE html>
<html>
<head>
```

```html
<style>
p.normal {
   font-style: normal;
}
p.italic {
   font-style: italic;
}
p.oblique {
   font-style: oblique;
}
</style>
</head>
<body>
<p class="normal"> You can see Normal style paragraph.</p>
<p class="italic">You can see italic style paragraph.</p>
<p class="oblique">You can see oblique style paragraph.</p>
</body>
</html>
```

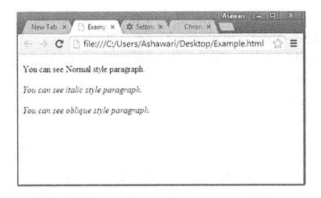

Font Size

The font-size property is used to set the size of the text. It is important to know how to set the size of the text in proper manner. The size of the font can be specified in several ways. We will look t them in details one by one.

Pixels

Pixels are commonly used to control the font size of the text. As they offer precise control over the font size, web designers generally use pixels. The number of pixels is followed by letters px.

Percentages

The 100 % size corresponds to 16px. Hence, 12px makes 75% and 200% corresponds to 32px. If you create a rule to make the text inside the <body> element to be 75% of the default size it would be 12px. And if you take another element inside the body element and make its size 75%, it would be 9px.(75% of 12px). Thus percentages work in setting font size. It is called as relative size setting.

Ems

Ems are equivalent to width of the letter 'm'. 'em' can be used to resize the text in the browser. Hence it is used by many developers. 1em is equivalent to 16px. So size in 'em' can be calculated using the formula pixels/16=em.

```
<!DOCTYPE html>
<html>
<head>
<style>
body {
    font-size: 16px;
}
h1 {
    font-style: 200%;
}
h2 {
    font-style: 1.3em;
}
```

```
</style>
</head>
<body>
<p> This is Normal text</p>
<h1>Heading1</p>
<h2>Heading2</p>
</body>
</html>
```

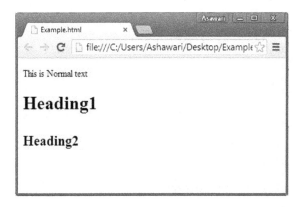

n the above example, the basic normal font of the browser is set at 16 px. And font sizes for heading1 and heading2 are set relative to the basic font.

Font Weight

The font-weight property can be used to create the bold font. It specifies how much bold font is.

There are some values of this property like, normal, bold, bolder, lighter, 100, 200, 300, 400, 500, 600, 700, 800, 900 etc. Following example describes the values of the property.

```
<!DOCTYPE html>
<html>
<head>
<style>
p.bold{
    font-weight:bold;
}
p.bolder{
    font-weight:bolder;
}
p.lighter{
    font-weight: lighter;
}
p.hundred{
    font-weight: 100;
}
p.fivehundred{
    font-weight: 500;
}
p.ninehundred{
```

```
    font-weight: 900;
}
</style>
</head>
<body>
<p class="bold"> This is bold text</p>
<p class="bolder"> This is bolder text</p>
<p class="lighter"> This is lighter text</p>
<p class="hundred"> This is 100 times bold
text</p>
<p class="fivehundred"> This is 500 times bold
text</p>
<p class="ninehundred"> This is 900 times bold
text</p>
</body>
</html>
```

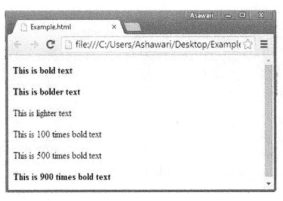

Chapter 13:
Background

Background effects can be added with the help of CSS style rules. There are various style rules which make the background attractive. We will look at all those properties in this chapter.

Background color

The background-color property sets the background color of the element.he background color of the page is set as follows.

body { background-color: pink}

Different background colors can also be applied to different elements.

```
<!DOCTYPE html>
<html>
<head>
<style>

h1 {
    background-color: Bisque;
}
```

```
p {
    background-color: BurlyWood;
}
div {
    background-color: #b0c4de;
}
</style>
</head>
<body>
<h1>HEADING BACKGROUND COLOR!</h1>
<div>
We wre inside div element
<p>This is normal paragraph with its own
background color.</p>
div element color will still be applied here
</div>
</body>
</html>
```

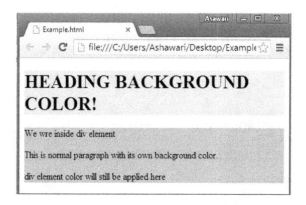

Background Image

The background-image property is used to specify the image as a background of the web page or HTML element. By default the image covers the entire element by being repeated. The background image of the page can be applied like this.

```
<!DOCTYPE html>
<html>
<head>
<style>
body {
    background-image: url("SoftBlue.jpg");
}
</style>
</head>
```

```
<body>
<h1>Hello World!</h1>
</body>
</html>
```

The background image should be chosen in such a way that the text on the image is readable.

Horizontal or vertical repeat

The background-repeat property sets the image horizontally or vertically. 'repeat-x' value sets the image horizontally and 'repeat-y' value sets the image vertically. If the repeat is not applied correctly the background will not look good.

```
<!DOCTYPE html>
<html>
<head>
```

```
<style>
body {
    background-image:
url("Lenovo_Autumn.jpg");
    background-repeat: repeat-y;
}
h1{
    color: white;
}
</style>
</head>
<body>
<h1>Hello World!</h1>
</body>
</html>
```

<!DOCTYPE html>

<html>

<head>

<style>

body {

  background-image:
url("Lenovo_Autumn.jpg");

  background-repeat: repeat-x;

}

h1{

  color: white;

}

```
</style>
</head>
<body>
<h1>Hello World!</h1>
</body>
</html>
```

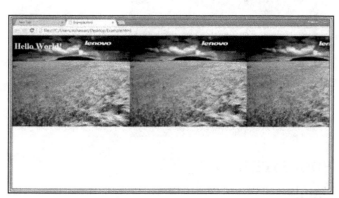

ss

If you do not want the image to be repeated you can set the value of the background-repeat property as "no-repeat"

Background Image position

When an image is not being repeated you can use the background-position property to specify the position of the image in the browser window. It has a pair of values. The first represent the horizontal position and second represent vertical position. The probable values are left top, left center, left bottom, center top, center bottom, center center, right top, right bottom, right center etc. You can even set the position in pixel percentages. The top left corner is 0%0%. Corresponding percentages are calculated taking this as a reference. With values as 50%50% centers the image horizontally and vertically.

```
<!DOCTYPE html>
<html>
<head>
<style>
body {
    background-image: url("logo.png");
    background-repeat: no-repeat;
    background-position: 100px 100px;
}
</style>
</head>
<body>
<h1>Hello World!</h1>
</body>
</html>
```

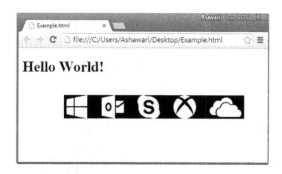

Background Attachment

The background-attachment determines whether the image is fixed or scrolls with the rest of the page. The values of this property are fixed or scroll. Following example states how to set the fixed background image.

h1{

    background-image: url("Stars.jpg");

    background-repeat: no-repeat;

    background-attachment: fixed;

}

Following example states how to set the scrolling background image.

h1{

    background-image: url("Stars.jpg");

    background-repeat: no-repeat;

    background-attachment: scroll;

}

Background Shorthand

There are many properties to deal with while setting background. You can use the background property to set all the background properties at once. It is mainly used to shorten the code.

When using the shorthand property the order of the property values is:

1. background-color
2. background-image
3. background-repeat
4. background-attachment
5. background-position

It does not matter if one of the property values is missing, as long as the ones that are present are in this order.

```
body {
    background: Acqua url("Stars.png") no-repeat
fixed right top;
}
```

Chapter 14:
Lists, Links, Tables

We have seen how to create lists with the help of HTML elements. To configure the numbered or bullet points CSS can be used. The list position and style can be controlled using CSS. We will see such CSS properties in detail.

List Style Types

The list-style-type property can be used to configure the type of list item. Some of the values of this property are for unordered lists and some are for ordered lists. They are as follows.

Unordered List:

Value	Description
None	NA
disc (default)	A filled-in circle
Circle	An empty circle
Square	A filled-in square

Value	Description	Example
decimal	Number	1,2,3,4,5
decimal-leading-	0 before the number	01, 02, 03,
lower-alpha	Lowercase alphanumeric characters	a, b, c, d, e
upper-alpha	Uppercase alphanumeric characters	A, B, C, D,
lower-roman	Lowercase Roman numerals	i, ii, iii, iv, v
upper-roman	Uppercase Roman numerals	I, II, III,
lower-greek	The marker is lower-greek	alpha, beta,
lower-latin	The marker is lower-latin	a, b, c, d, e
upper-latin	The marker is upper-latin	A, B, C, D,
hebrew	The marker is traditional Hebrew numbering	
armenian	The marker is traditional Armenian numbering	
georgian	The marker is traditional Georgian numbering	
cjk-ideographic	The marker is plain ideographic numbers	
hiragana	The marker is hiragana	a, i, u, e, o,
katakana	The marker is katakana	A, I, U, E,
hiragana-iroha	The marker is hiragana-iroha	i, ro, ha, ni,
katakana-iroha	The marker is katakana-iroha	I, RO, HA,

```html
<html>
  <head>
  </head>
    <body>
    <ul style="list-style-type:circle;">
      <li>Maths</li>
      <li>Social Science</li>
      <li>Physics</li>
    </ul>
```

```html
    <ul style="list-style-type:square;">
    <li>Maths</li>
    <li>Social Science</li>
    <li>Physics</li>
  </ul>
    <ol style="list-style-type:decimal;">
    <li>Maths</li>
    <li>Social Science</li>
    <li>Physics</li>
  </ol>
    <ol style="list-style-type:lower-alpha;">
    <li>Maths</li>
    <li>Social Science</li>
    <li>Physics</li>
  </ol>
    <ol style="list-style-type:lower-roman;">
    <li>Maths</li>
    <li>Social Science</li>
    <li>Physics</li>
  </ol>
</body>
</html>
```

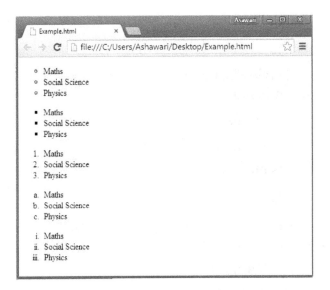

The List Style position

The list-style-position property sets the position of the marker. The position can be inside or outside the box where the items are listed. In case of 'inside' value, if the text goes onto a second line, the text will wrap underneath the marker. It will also appear indented to where the text would have started if the list had a value of outside. In case of 'outside' value, if the text goes onto a second line, the text will be aligned with the start of the first line (to the right of the bullet).

<html>
  <head>

```html
</head>
<body>
    <ul style="list-style-type:square;list-style-
position:inside;">
        <li>Maths</li>
        <li>Social Science</li>
        <li>Physics</li>
    </ul>
    <ol style="list-style-type:decimal;list-style-
position:outside;">
        <li>Maths</li>
        <li>Social Science</li>
        <li>Physics</li>
    </ol>
</body>
</html>
```

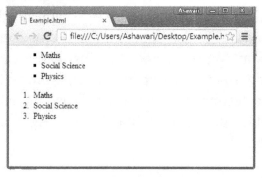

The list style image

An image can be set as a list item marker with the help of the property list-style-image. In this way you can have your own bullets for the list. The value is given as bullet file under the url tag. Syntax is shown below.

```
ul {
    list-style-image: url('sqpurple.gif');
}
```

If it does not find the given bullet file, default bullet is shown.

```
<!DOCTYPE html>
<html>
<head>
<style>
ul {
    list-style-image: url('arrow-right.gif');
}
li {
    font-size:24px;
}
</style>
</head>
```

```
<body>
<ul>
  <li>Coffee</li>
  <li>Tea</li>
  <li>Coca Cola</li>
</ul>
</body>
</html>
```

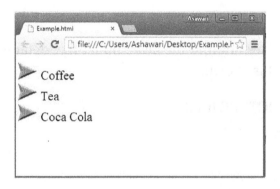

List-shorthand property

The list-style property can be used to set all the list properties in one go. No need to set the list styles individually. Syntax is as follows.

```
ul {
    list-style: square inside url("arrow-right.gif");
}
```

When using the shorthand property, the order of the property values is as follows:

list-style-type (if a list-style-image is specified, the value of this property will be displayed if the image for some reason cannot be displayed)

list-style-position (specifies whether the list-item markers should appear inside or outside the content flow)

list-style-image (specifies an image as the list item marker)

If one of the property values above is missing, the default value for the missing property will be inserted, if any.

Marker Offset

The distance between the marker and the text in front of it can be adjusted using marker-offset property. It's value should be in length preferably ems.

```
<html>
  <head>
  </head>

  <body>
```

```
<ul style="list-style: inside square;">
  <li>Maths</li>
  <li>Social Science</li>
  <li>Physics</li>
</ul>

<ol style="list-style: outside upper-alpha;">
  <li>Maths</li>
  <li>Social Science</li>
  <li>Physics</li>
</ol>
</body>

</html>
```

Styling Links

In the HTML part we have seen how to establish various types of links. Now we will see how to style those links with the help of CSS. Links can be styled with various CSS properties linke color, font-family, background etc. So apply those properties to HTML element 'a'.

```
<!DOCTYPE html>
<html>
```

```html
<head>
<style>
a {
    color: #FFF000;
}
</style>
</head>
<body>
<p><b><a href="ABC.asp"
target="_blank">Linking The
World!</a></b></p>
</body>
</html>
```

For different states, the links can be styled. For e.g. like active link,visited link etc. You can choose to style it as per your own choice of colors, fonts etc.

These states are as follows.

a:link - a normal, unvisited link

a:visited - a link the user has visited

a:hover - a link when the user rolls mouse over it

a:active - a link the moment it is clicked

```html
<!DOCTYPE html>
<html>
<head>
<style>
/* unvisited link */
a:link {
    color: #FF0000;
}
/* visited link */
a:visited {
    color: #00FF00;
}
/* mouse over link */
a:hover {
    color: #FF00FF;
}
/* selected link */
a:active {
    color: #0000FF;
}
</style>
</head>
<body>
```

```html
<p><b><a href="default.asp"
target="_blank">This is a link</a></b></p>
```

While setting these states of links, there is a rule

a:hover MUST come after a:link and a:visited

a:active MUST come after a:hover

There are other styles of the linking like text-decoration and background color etc wich are commonly used. To change the background color of the link the background-color property can be applied to different states of the link.

```html
<!DOCTYPE html>
<html>
<head>
<style>
a:link {
    background-color: #B2FF99;
}

a:visited {
    background-color: #FFFF85;
}

a:hover {
```

```
    background-color: #FF704D;
}


a:active {
    background-color: #FF704D;
}
</style>
</head>
<body>
```

To remove underline of the link, text-decoration property can be used.

```
<!DOCTYPE html>
<html>
<head>
<style>
a:link {
    text-decoration: none;
}


a:visited {
    text-decoration: none;
}
```

```css
a:hover {
    text-decoration: underline;
}

a:active {
    text-decoration: underline;
}
</style>
</head>
<body>

<p><b><a href="default.asp"
target="_blank">This is a link</a></b></p>
</body>
</html>
```

This is all about the links as of now. We will revisit the same properties when we see the psudo-classes.

Styling Tables

You can style the tables using CSS rules. Like this you can make tables impressive enough to read. We will see setting different properties for the HTML table in order to decorate it.

Table Borders

Set the borders of the table using the 'border' property. Following example shows how to specify black color border to the <table>, <th> and <td> elements

```
<!DOCTYPE html>
<html>
<head>
<style>
table, th, td {
    border: 1px solid black;
}
</style>
</head>
<body>

<table>
  <tr>
    <th>Firstname</th>
    <th>Lastname</th>
  </tr>
  <tr>
    <td>Peter</td>
```

```
    <td>Griffin</td>
  </tr>
  <tr>
    <td>Lois</td>
    <td>Griffin</td>
  </tr>
</table>
</body>
</html>
```

Above example shows double border around the table elements. This is because the border is applied to table as well as table elements. For removal of double borders you can use border collapse property described below.

Borders Collapse

The border-collapse border is used to specify whether the table borders should be collapsed into single border.

```
<!DOCTYPE html>
<html>
<head>
<style>
table {
```

```
    border-collapse: collapse;
}
table, td, th {
    border: 1px solid black;
}
</style>
</head>
<body>
<table>
  <tr>
    <th>Firstname</th>
    <th>Lastname</th>
  </tr>
  <tr>
    <td>Asawari</td>
    <td>Pachkhede</td>
  </tr>
  <tr>
    <td>Sameer</td>
    <td>Pachkhede</td>
  </tr>
</table>
</body>
</html>
```

Table Width and Height

Width and height properties specify the width and height of the table.

```
table {
    width: 100%;
}
th {
    height: 50px;
}
```

In above example the table width has been specified at 100% and height as 50 pixels. With the trial and error you can adjust these values. Once you get an estimation of the height and width values you will be able to set these values quickly.

Horizontal and Vertical Alignment

The text-align property is used to set the horizontal alignment of the text within the cell like left, right or center. By default the <th> element has center alignment and <td> element has left alignment. We can change these values as per our own needs. The vertical-align property can be set to make the text vertically aligned as top, bottom or middle. By default the vertical alignment for the table elements is middle.

```
<!DOCTYPE html>
<html>
<head>
<style>
table, td, th {
    border: 1px solid black;
}
table {
    width: 100%;
}
th {
    text-align: left;
}
td {
    height: 50px;
    vertical-align: bottom;
}
</style>
</head>
<body>
```

```
<table>
 <tr>
  <th>Firstname</th>
  <th>Lastname</th>
  <th>Savings</th>
 </tr>
 <tr>
  <td>Peter</td>
  <td>Griffin</td>
  <td>$100</td>
 </tr>
 <tr>
  <td>Lois</td>
  <td>Griffin</td>
  <td>$150</td>
 </tr>
 <tr>
  <td>Joe</td>
  <td>Swanson</td>
  <td>$300</td>
 </tr>
 <tr>
  <td>Cleveland</td>
  <td>Brown</td>
```

```
      <td>$250</td>
   </tr>
   </table>
   </body>
   </html>
```

Padding

To control the space between border and content, padding property can be set. Set the values for this property for <td> and <th> element. Example shown below.

```
<style>
table, td, th {
   border: 1px solid black;
}
td {
   padding: 15px;
}
</style>
```

The Border Spacing

The border-spacing property specifies the distance that separates adjacent cells' borders. It can take either one or two values; these should be units of length.

If you provide one value, it will apply to both vertical and horizontal borders. Or you can specify two values, in which case, the first refers to the horizontal spacing and the second to the vertical spacing.

```
<html>
  <head>

    <style type="text/css">
      table.one {
        border-collapse:separate;
        width:400px;
        border-spacing:10px;
      }
      table.two {
        border-collapse:separate;
        width:400px;
        border-spacing:10px 50px;
      }
    </style>

  </head>
  <body>
```

```
<table class="one" border="1">

    <caption>Separate Border Example with
border-spacing</caption>

    <tr><td> Cell A Collapse
Example</td></tr>

    <tr><td> Cell B Collapse
Example</td></tr>

    </table>

    <br />


    <table class="two" border="1">

    <caption>Separate Border Example with
border-spacing</caption>

    <tr><td> Cell A Separate
Example</td></tr>

    <tr><td> Cell B Separate
Example</td></tr>

    </table>


  </body>
</html>
```

The Caption side

The caption-side property allows you to specify
where the content of a <caption> element should

be placed in relationship to the table. The table that follows lists the possible values.

This property can have one of the four values top, bottom, left or right. The following example uses each value.

```
<html>
  <head>

    <style type="text/css">
      caption.top {caption-side:top}
      caption.bottom {caption-side:bottom}
      caption.left {caption-side:left}
      caption.right {caption-side:right}
    </style>

  </head>
  <body>

    <table style="width:400px; border:1px solid black;">
      <caption class="top">
      This caption will appear at the top
      </caption>
      <tr><td > Cell A</td></tr>
```

```
<tr><td > Cell B</td></tr>
</table>
<br />


<table style="width:400px; border:1px solid
black;">
    <caption class="bottom">
    This caption will appear at the bottom
    </caption>
    <tr><td > Cell A</td></tr>
    <tr><td > Cell B</td></tr>
</table>
<br />


<table style="width:400px; border:1px solid
black;">
    <caption class="left">
    This caption will appear at the left
    </caption>
    <tr><td > Cell A</td></tr>
    <tr><td > Cell B</td></tr>
</table>
<br />
```

```
<table style="width:400px; border:1px solid
black;">
    <caption class="right">
    This caption will appear at the right
    </caption>
    <tr><td > Cell A</td></tr>
    <tr><td > Cell B</td></tr>
   </table>

  </body>
</html>
```

Empty Cells Property

The empty-cells property indicates whether a cell without any content should have a border displayed.

This property can have one of the three values - show, hide or inherit.

Here is the empty-cells property used to hide borders of empty cells in the <table> element.

```
<html>
  <head>
   <style type="text/css">
    table.empty{
```

```
      width:350px;
      border-collapse:separate;
      empty-cells:hide;
    }
    td.empty{
      padding:5px;
      border-style:solid;
      border-width:1px;
      border-color:#999999;
    }
  </style>

</head>
<body>

  <table class="empty">
  <tr>
    <th></th>
    <th>Title one</th>
    <th>Title two</th>
  </tr>

  <tr>
    <th>Row Title</th>
```

```html
    <td class="empty">value</td>
    <td class="empty">value</td>
  </tr>

  <tr>
    <th>Row Title</th>
    <td class="empty">value</td>
    <td class="empty"></td>
  </tr>
  </table>
  </body>
</html>
```

The Table Layout

The table-layout property is supposed to help you control how a browser should render or lay out a table.This property can have one of the three values: fixed, auto or inherit. The following example shows the difference between these properties.

```html
<html>
  <head>

    <style type="text/css">
```

```
    table.auto {
      table-layout: auto
    }
    table.fixed{
      table-layout: fixed
    }
  </style>

  </head>
  <body>

    <table class="auto" border="1"
width="100%">
    <tr>
      <td
width="20%">100000000000000000000000
0000</td>
      <td width="40%">10000000</td>
      <td width="40%">100</td>
    </tr>
    </table>
    <br />

    <table class="fixed" border="1"
width="100%">
```

```html
<tr>

<td width="20%">100000000000000000000000
0000</td>

<td width="40%">10000000</td>

<td width="40%">100</td>

</tr>

</table>


</body>
</html>
```

Chapter 15:
Boxes

According to the box model concept, every element on a page is a rectangular box and may have width, height, padding, borders, and margins. Every element on every page conforms to the box model, so it's incredibly important. Let's take a look at it, along with a few new CSS properties, to better understand what we are working with.

Every element is a rectangular box, and there are several properties that determine the size of that box. The core of the box is defined by the width and height of an element, which may be determined by the display property, by the contents of the element, or by specified width and height properties. padding a nd then border expand the dimensions of the box outward from the element's width and height. Lastly, any marginwe have specified will follow the border.

Each part of the box model corresponds to a CSS property: width, height, padding, border, and margin.

Let's look these properties inside some code:

```
div {
  border: 6px solid #949599;
  height: 100px;
  margin: 20px;
  padding: 20px;
  width: 400px;
}
```

According to the box model, the total width of an element can be calculated using the following formula:

margin-right + border-right + padding-right + width + padding-left + border-left + margin-left

In comparison, according to the box model, the total height of an element can be calculated using the following formula:

margin-top + border-top + padding-top + height + padding-bottom + border-bottom + margin-bottom

Using the formulas, we can find the total height and width of our example code.

Width: 492px = 20px + 6px + 20px + 400px + 20px + 6px + 20px

Height: 192px = 20px + 6px + 20px + 100px + 20px + 6px + 20px

The box model is without question one of the more confusing parts of HTML and CSS. We set a width property value of 400 pixels, but the actual width of our element is 492pixels. By default the box model is additive; thus to determine the actual size of a box we need to take into account padding, borders, and margins for all four sides of the box. Our width not only includes the width property value, but also the size of the left and right padding, left and right borders, and left and right margins.

So far a lot of these properties might not make a whole lot of sense, and that's all right. To clarify things, let's take a close look at all of the properties—width, height,padding, border, and margin—that go into forming the box model.

Width & Height

Every element has default width and height. That width and height may be 0 pixels, but browsers, by default, will render every element with size. Depending on how an element is displayed, the default width and height may be adequate. If an element is key to the layout of a page, it may require   specified width and height property values. In this case, the property values for non-inline elements may be specified.

Width

The default width of an element depends on its display value. Block-level elements have a default width of 100%, consuming the entire horizontal space available. Inline and inline-block elements expand and contract horizontally to accommodate their content. Inline-level elements cannot have a fixed size, thus the width and heightproperties are only relevant to non-inline elements. To set a specific width for a non-inline element, use the width property:

div {

  width: 400px;

}

Height

The default height of an element is determined by its content. An element will expand and contract vertically as necessary to accommodate its content. To set a specific height for a non-inline element, use the height property:

```
div {
  height: 100px;
}
```

Margin & Padding

Depending on the element, browsers may apply
default margins and padding to an element to
help with legibility and clarity. We will generally
see this with text-based elements. The default
margins and padding for these elements may
differ from browser to browser and element to
element.

Margin

The margin property allows us to set the amount
of space that surrounds an element. Margins for
an element fall outside of any border and are
completely transparent in color. Margins can be
used to help position elements in a particular
place on a page or to provide breathing room,
keeping all other elements a safe distance away.
Here's the margin property in action:

```
div {
  margin: 20px;
}
```

One oddity with the margin property is that vertical margins, top and bottom, are not accepted by inline-level elements. These vertical margins are, however, accepted by block-level and inline-block elements.

```html
<html>
  <head>
  </head>
  <body>
    <p style="margin: 15px; border:1px solid black;">

    all four margins will be 15px

    </p>
    <p style="margin:10px 2%; border:1px solid black;">

    top and bottom margin will be 10px, left and right margin will be 2% of the total width of the document.

    </p>
    <p style="margin: 10px 2% -10px; border:1px solid black;">

    top margin will be 10px, left and right margin will be 2% of the total width of the document, bottom margin will be -10px

    </p>
```

```
<p style="margin: 10px 2% -10px auto;
border:1px solid black;">
```

top margin will be 10px, right margin will be 2% of the total width of the document, bottom margin will be -10px, left margin will be set by the browser

```
</p>
</body>
</html>
```

Padding

The padding property is very similar to the margin property; however, it falls inside of an element's border, should an element have a border. The padding property is used to provide spacing directly within an element. Here's the code:

```
div {
  padding: 20px;
}
```

The padding property, unlike the margin property, works vertically on inline-level elements. This vertical padding may blend into the line above or below the given element, but it will be displayed.

```html
<html>
  <head>
  </head>

  <body>
    <p style="padding: 15px; border:1px solid black;">
    all four padding will be 15px
    </p>


    <p style="padding:10px 2%; border:1px solid black;">
    top and bottom padding will be 10px, left and right
    padding will be 2% of the total width of the document.
    </p>


    <p style="padding: 10px 2% 10px; border:1px solid black;">
    top padding will be 10px, left and right padding will
    be 2% of the total width of the document, bottom padding will be 10px
    </p>
```

```
    <p style="padding: 10px 2% 10px 10px;
border:1px solid black;">

    top padding will be 10px, right padding will
be 2% of

    the total width of the document, bottom
padding and top padding will be 10px

    </p>
  </body>


</html>
```

Margin & Padding Declarations

In CSS, there is more than one way to declare
values for certain properties. We can use
longhand, listing multiple properties and values
one after the other, in which each value has its
own property. Or we can use shorthand, listing
multiple values with one property. Not all
properties have a shorthand alternative, so we
must make sure we are using the correct
property and value structure.

The margin and padding properties come in both
longhand and shorthand form. When using the
shorthand margin property to set the same value
for all four sides of an element, we specify one
value:

```
div {
  margin: 20px;
}
```

To set one value for the top and bottom and another value for the left and right sides of an element, specify two values: top and bottom first, then left and right. Here we are placing margins of 10 pixels on the top and bottom of a <div> and margins of 20 pixels on the left and right:

```
div {
  margin: 10px 20px;
}
```

To set unique values for all four sides of an element, specify those values in the order of top, right, bottom, and left, moving clockwise. Here we are placing margins of 10 pixels on the top of a <div>, 20 pixels on the right, 0 pixels on the bottom, and 15 pixels on the left.

```
div {
  margin: 10px 20px 0 15px;
}
```

Using the margin or padding property alone, with any number of values, is considered shorthand. With longhand, we can set the value for one side at a time using unique properties. Each property name (in this case margin or padding) is followed by a dash and the side of the box to which the value is to be applied: top, right, bottom, or left. For example, the padding-left property accepts only one value and will set the left padding for that element; the margin-top property accepts only one value and will set the top margin for that element.

```
div {
  margin-top: 10px;
  padding-left: 6px;
}
```

When we wish to identify only one margin or padding value, it is best to use the longhand properties. Doing so keeps our code explicit and helps us to avoid any confusion down the road. For example, did we really want to set the top, right, and left sides of the element to have margins of 0 pixels, or did we really only want to set the bottom margin to 10 pixels? Using longhand properties and values here helps to make our intentions clear. When dealing with three or more values, though, shorthand is incredibly helpful.

Borders

Borders fall between the padding and margin, providing an outline around an element. The border property requires three values: width, style, and color. Shorthand values for the border property are stated in that order— width, style, color. In longhand, these three values can be broken up into the border-width, border-style, and border-color properties. These longhand properties are useful for changing, or overwriting, a single border value.

The width and color of borders can be defined using common CSS units of length and color. Borders can have different appearances. The most common style values are solid, double, dashed, dotted, and none, but there are several others to choose from.

Here is the code for a 6-pixel-wide, solid, gray border that wraps around all four sides of a <div>:

```
div {
  border: 6px solid #949599;
}
```

The border-style Property

The border-style property allows you to select one of the following styles of border –

none: No border. (Equivalent of border-width:o;)

solid: Border is a single solid line.

dotted: Border is a series of dots.

dashed: Border is a series of short lines.

double: Border is two solid lines.

groove: Border looks as though it is carved into the page.

ridge: Border looks the opposite of groove.

inset: Border makes the box look like it is embedded in the page.

outset: Border makes the box look like it is coming out of the canvas.

hidden: Same as none, except in terms of border-conflict resolution for table elements.

You can individually change the style of the bottom, left, top, and right borders of an element using the following properties –

border-bottom-style changes the style of bottom border.

border-top-style changes the style of top border.

border-left-style changes the style of left border.

border-right-style changes the style of right border.

The following example shows all these border styles –

```
<html>
  <head>
  </head>
    <body>.
    <p style="border-width:4px; border-style:none;">
    This is a border with none width.
    </p>
    <p style="border-width:4px; border-style:solid;">
    This is a solid border.
    </p>
```

```
<p style="border-width:4px; border-
style:dashed;">
```

This is a dahsed border.

```
</p>
```

```
<p style="border-width:4px; border-
style:double;">
```

This is a double border.

```
</p>
```

```
<p style="border-width:4px; border-
style:groove;">
```

This is a groove border.

```
</p>
```

```
<p style="border-width:4px; border-
style:ridge">
```

This is aridge border.

```
</p>
```

```
<p style="border-width:4px; border-
style:inset;">
```

This is a inset border.

```
</p>
```

```
<p style="border-width:4px; border-
style:outset;">
```

This is a outset border.

```
</p>
```

```
<p style="border-width:4px; border-
style:hidden;">
```

This is a hidden border.

```
</p>
<p style="border-width:4px;border-top-style:solid;
```

```
border-bottom-style:dashed; border-left-style:groove; border-right-style:double;">
```

This is a a border with four different styles.

```
</p>
</body>
</html>
```

The border-width Property

The border-width property allows you to set the width of an element borders. The value of this property could be either a length in px, pt or cm or it should be set to thin, medium or thick.

You can individually change the width of the bottom, top, left, and right borders of an element using the following properties –

- border-bottom-width changes the width of bottom border.

- border-top-width changes the width of top border.

- border-left-width changes the width of left border.

- border-right-width changes the width of right border.

Individual Border Sides

As with the margin and padding properties, borders can be placed on one side of an element at a time if we'd like. Doing so requires new properties: border-top, border-right, border-bottom, and border-left. The values for these properties are the same as those of the border property alone: width, style, and color. If we want, we can make a border appear only on the bottom of an element:

```
div {
  border-bottom: 6px solid #949599;
}
```

Additionally, styles for individual border sides may be controlled at an even finer level. For example, if we wish to change only the width of the bottom border we can use the following code:

```
div {
  border-bottom-width: 12px;
}
```

These highly specific longhand border properties include a series of hyphen-separated words starting with the border base, followed by the selected side—top, right,bottom, or left—and then width, style, or color, depending on the desired property.

Border Radius

While we're looking at borders and their different properties, we need to examine the border-radius property, which enables us to round the corners of an element.

The border-radius property accepts length units, including percentages and pixels, that identify the radius by which the corners of an element are to be rounded. A single value will round all four corners of an element equally; two values will round the top-left/bottom-right and top-right/bottom-left corners in that order; four values will round the top-left, top-right, bottom-right, and bottom-left corners in that order.

When considering the order in which multiple values are applied to the border-radiusproperty (as well as the margin and padding properties), remember that they move in a clockwise fashion starting at the top left of an element.

```
div {
  border-radius: 5px;
}
```

The border-radius property may also be broken out into longhand properties that allow us to change the radii of individual corners of an element. These longhand properties begin with border, continue with the corner's vertical location (top orbottom) and the corner's horizontal location (left or right), and then end with radius. For example, to change the top-right corner radius of a <div>, the border-top-right-radius property can be used.

Border Properties Using Shorthand

The border property allows you to specify color, style, and width of lines in one property. The following example shows how to use all the three properties into a single property. This is the most frequently used property to set border around any element.

```
<html>
  <head>
  </head>
  <body>
    <p style="border:4px solid red;">
    This example is showing shorthand property
for border.
    </p>
  </body>
```

</html>

Box Sizing

Until now the box model has been an additive design. If you set the width of an element to 400 pixels and then add 20 pixels of padding and a border of 10 pixels on every side, the actual full width of the element becomes 460 pixels. Remember, we need to add the width, padding, and border property values together to get the actual, full width of an element.

The box model may, however, be changed to support different calculations. CSS3 introduced the box-sizing property, which allows us to change exactly how the box model works and how an element's size is calculated. The property accepts three primary values—content-box, padding-box, and border-box—each of which has a slightly different impact on how the box size is calculated.

Content Box

The content-box value is the default value, leaving the box model as an additive design. If we don't use the box-sizing property, this will be the default value for all elements. The size of an element begins with the width and height properties, and then any padding, border, or margin property values are added on from there.

```
div {
  -webkit-box-sizing: content-box;
    -moz-box-sizing: content-box;
      box-sizing: content-box;
}
```

Padding Box

The padding-box value alters the box model by including any padding property values within the width and height of an element. When using the padding-box value, if an element has a width of 400 pixels and a padding of 20 pixels around every side, the actual width will remain 400 pixels. As any padding values increase, the content size within an element shrinks proportionately.

If we add a border or margin, those values will be added to the width or heightproperties to calculate the full box size. For example, if we add a border of 10 pixels and a padding of 20 pixels around every side of the element with a width of 400 pixels, the actual full width will become 420 pixels.

```
div {
  box-sizing: padding-box;
}
```

Border Box

Lastly, the border-box value alters the box model so that any border or paddingproperty values are included within the width and height of an element. When using the border-box value, if an element has a width of 400 pixels, a padding of 20 pixels around every side, and a border of 10 pixels around every side, the actual width will remain 400 pixels.

If we add a margin, those values will need to be added to calculate the full box size. No matter which box-sizing property value is used, any margin values will need to be added to calculate the full size of the element.

```
div {
  box-sizing: border-box;
}
```

Picking a Box Size

Generally speaking, the best box-sizing value to use is border-box. The border-boxvalue makes our math much, much easier. If we want an element to be 400 pixels wide, it is, and it will remain 400 pixels wide no matter what padding or border values we add to it.

Additionally, we can easily mix length values. Say we want our box to be 40% wide. Adding a padding of 20 pixels and a border of 10 pixels around every side of an element isn't difficult, and we can still guarantee that the actual width of our box will remain 40% despite using pixel values elsewhere.

The only drawback to using the box-sizing property is that as part of the CSS3 specification, it isn't supported in every browser; it especially lacks support in older browsers. Fortunately this is becoming less and less relevant as new browsers are released. Chances are we're safe to use the box-sizing property, but should we notice any issues, it's worth looking into which browser those issues are occurring with.

Chapter 16:
Layout

In this chapter we are going to learn how to fix the various controls on the web page and make the layout look attractive. Layout can be controlled and controls can be positioned using CSS. So knowing how to do it will get you an edge in web designing.

Block level and Inline level Elements

The block level boxes start on a new line and act as the main building blocks of any layout, while inline boxes flow between surrounding text. You can control how much space each box takes up by setting the width of the boxes. To separate boxes, you can use borders, margins, paddings and background colors.

Examples of block-level elements:

- <div>
- <h1> - <h6>
- <p>
- <form>
- <header>

- <footer>
- <section>

Examples of inline elements:

- <span>
- <a>
- <img>

The display property

The display property specifies if/how an element is displayed. Every HTML element has a default display value depending on what type of element it is. The default display value for most elements is block or inline. display: none; is commonly used with JavaScript to hide and show elements without deleting and recreating them. The <script> element use display: none; as its default.

Changing an inline element to a block element, or vice versa, can be useful for making the page look a specific way, and still follow the web standards. A common example is making inline <li> elements for horizontal menus:

```
li {

  display: inline;

}
```

Hiding an element can be done by setting the display property to none. The element will be hidden, and the page will be displayed as if the element is not there. visibility: hidden; also hides an element. However, the element will still take up the same space as before. The element will be hidden, but still affect the layout:

```
<!DOCTYPE html>
<html>
<head>
<style>
h1.hidden {
  display: none;
}
</style>
</head>
<body>

<h1>This is a visible heading</h1>
<h1 class="hidden">This is a hidden heading</h1>
```

```
<p>Notice that the h1 element with display:
none; does not take up any space.</p>
</body>
```

```
<!DOCTYPE html>
<html>
<head>
<style>
h1.hidden {
    visibility: hidden;
}
</style>
</head>
<body>

<h1>This is a visible heading</h1>
<h1 class="hidden">This is a hidden
heading</h1>
<p>Notice that the hidden heading still takes up
space.</p>
</body>
```

CSS Positioning

CSS helps you to position your HTML element.
You can put any HTML element at whatever

location you like. You can specify whether you want the element positioned relative to its natural position in the page or absolute based on its parent element.

Relative Positioning

Relative positioning changes the position of the HTML element relative to where it normally appears. So "left:20" adds 20 pixels to the element's LEFT position. You can use two values top and left along   with the position property to move an HTML element anywhere in the HTML document.

- Move Left - Use a negative value for left.
- Move Right - Use a positive value for left.
- Move Up - Use a negative value for top.
- Move Down - Use a positive value for top.

You can use bottom or right values as well in the same way as top andleft.

```
<html>
  <head>
  </head>
  <body>
```

```
<div
style="position:relative;left:80px;top:2px;backgr
ound-color:yellow;">

This div has relative positioning.

</div>

</body>

</html>
```

Absolute Positioning

An element with position: absolute is positioned at the specified coordinates relative to your screen top-left corner. You can use two values top and left along   with the position property to move an HTML element anywhere in the HTML document.

- Move Left - Use a negative value for left.
- Move Right - Use a positive value for left.
- Move Up - Use a negative value for top.
- Move Down - Use a positive value for top.

You can use bottom or right values as well in the same way as top and left.

Here is an example –

```
<html>
  <head>
```

```
</head>
<body>
   <div style="position:absolute; left:80px;
top:20px; background-color:yellow;">
   This div has absolute positioning.
   </div>
   </body>
</html>
```

Fixed Positioning

Fixed positioning allows you to fix the position
of an element to a particular spot on the page,
regardless of scrolling. Specified coordinates will
be relative to the browser window. You can use
two   values top and left along   with
the position property to move an HTML element
anywhere in the HTML document.

- Move Left - Use a negative value for left.
- Move Right - Use a positive value for left.
- Move Up - Use a negative value for top.
- Move Down - Use a positive value for top.

You can use bottom or right values as well in the
same way as top andleft.

```
<html>
  <head>
  </head>
  <body>
    <div style="position:fixed; left:80px;
top:20px; background-color:yellow;">

    This div has fixed positioning.

    </div>
  </body>
</html>
```

Static Positioning

HTML elements are positioned static by default. Static positioned elements are not affected by the top, bottom, left, and right properties. An element with position: static; is not positioned in any special way; it is always positioned according to the normal flow of the page.

```
<!DOCTYPE html>
<html>
<head>
<style>
div.static {
  position: static;
  border: 3px solid #8AC007;
```

```
}
</style>
</head>
<body>
<h2>position: static;</h2>
<p>An element with position: static; is not
positioned in any special way; it is
always positioned according to the normal flow
of the page:</p>
<div class="static">
This div element has position: static;
</div>
</body>
```

Overlapping Elements

When elements are positioned, they can overlap
other elements. The z-index property specifies
the stack order of an element (which element
should be placed in front of, or behind, the
others). An element can have a positive or
negative stack order. An element with greater
stack order is always in front of an element with
a lower stack order.

```
<!DOCTYPE html>
<html>
<head>
<style>
img {
    position: absolute;
    left: 0px;
    top: 0px;
    z-index: -1;
}
</style>
</head>
<body>
<h1>This is a heading</h1>
<img src="w3css.gif" width="100"
height="140">
<p>Because the image has a z-index of -1, it will
be placed behind the text.</p>
</body>
```

Float and Clear

The float property specifies whether or not an element should float. The clear property is used to control the behavior of floating elements. In its simplest use, the float property can be used to wrap text around images. The following example specifies that an image should float to the right in a text:

```
img {
    float: right;
    margin: 0 0 10px 10px;
}
```

The clear property is used to control the behavior of floating elements. Elements after a floating element will flow around it. To avoid this, use the clear property. The clear property specifies on which sides of an element floating elements are not allowed to float:

```
div {
    clear: left;
}
```

If an element is taller than the element containing it, and it is floated, it will overflow outside of its container. Then we can add overflow: auto; to the containing element to fix this problem:

```
.clearfix {
    overflow: auto;
}
```

Layout Width and Max-Width

A block-level element always takes up the full width available (stretches out to the left and right as far as it can). Setting the width of a block-level element will prevent it from stretching out to the edges of its container. Then, you can set the margins to auto, to horizontally center the element within its container. The element will take up the specified width, and the remaining space will be split equally between the two margins.

Note: The problem with the <div> above occurs when the browser window is smaller than the width of the element. The browser then adds a horizontal scrollbar to the page.

Using max-width instead, in this situation, will improve the browser's handling of small windows. This is important when making a site usable on small devices:

```
<!DOCTYPE html>
<html>
<head>
<style>
div.ex1 {
   width:500px;
```

```
    margin: auto;
    border: 3px solid #8AC007;
}

div.ex2 {
    max-width:500px;
    margin: auto;
    border: 3px solid #8AC007;
}
</style>
</head>
<body>

<div class="ex1">This div element has width:
500px;</div>
<br>
<div class="ex2">This div element has max-
width: 500px;</div>
        </body>
```

Chapter 17:
Pseudo-elements and Pseudo class

In this chapter we will learn about the pseudo classes and pseudo elements.

Pseudo-Classes

A pseudo-class is similar to a class in HTML, but it's not specified explicitly in the markup. Some pseudo-classes are dynamic — they're applied as a result of user interaction with the document.

A pseudo-class starts with a colon (:). No whitespace may appear between a type selector or universal selector and the colon, nor can whitespace appear after the colon.

CSS1 introduced the :link, :visited, and :active pseudo-classes, but only for the HTML aelement. These pseudo-classes represented the state of links—unvisited, visited, or currently being selected—in a web page document. In CSS1, all three pseudo-classes were mutually exclusive.

CSS2 expanded the range of pseudo-classes and ensured that they could be applied to any element.:link and :visited now apply to any element defined as a link in the document language. While they remain mutually exclusive, the :active pseudo-class now joins :hover and :focus in the group of dynamic pseudo-classes. The :hover pseudo-class matches elements that are being designated by a pointing device (for example, elements that the user's hovering the cursor over);:active matches any element that's being activated by the user; and :focus matches any element that is currently in focus (that is, accepting input).

CSS2 also introduced the :lang pseudo-class to allow an element to be matched on the basis of its language, and the :first-child pseudo-class to match an element that's the first child element of its parent.CSS3 promises an even greater range of powerful pseudo-classes.

Remember that pseudo-classes, like ID selectors and attribute selectors, act like modifiers on type selectors and the universal selector: they specify additional constraints for the selector pattern, but they don't specify other elements. For instance, the selector li:first-child matches a list item that's the first child of its parent; it *doesn't* match the first child of a list item.

A simple selector can contain more than one pseudo-class if the pseudo-classes aren't mutually exclusive. For example, the selectors a:link:hover and a:visited:hover are valid, buta:link:visited isn't because :link and :visited are mutually exclusive. An element is either an unvisited link or a visited link.

The order of declaration is very important for the dynamic pseudo-classes :hover, :focus, and:active, depending on what you wish to achieve. The most commonly desired behavior for links is as follows:

a:link {

  : declarations

}

a:visited {

  : declarations

}

a:focus {

  : declarations

}

a:hover {

  : declarations

}

```
a:active {

  : declarations

}
```

The :link and :visited pseudo-classes   should generally come first. Next should be :focus and :hover they're specified now so that they override and apply to both visited and unvisited links. If :focus precedes :hover, the hover effect will apply to links with keyboard input focus. The: active pseudo-class should always come last, since we usually want to indicate clearly any links that have been activated.

This isn't the only useful order, nor is it in any way the "right" order. The order in which you specify your pseudo-classes will depend on the effects you want to show with different combinations of states. It's possible, for instance, that you might want to have different hover or focus effects on visited and unvisited links. In that case, you could combine pseudo-classes: a:link:hover.

If you want to apply special styling to the hover state of a link that also has keyboard input focus, use a:focus:hover.

The :link pseudo-class

The following example demonstrates how to use the :link class to set the link color. Possible values could be any color name in any valid format.

```
<html>
  <head>
    <style type="text/css">
      a:link {color:#000000}
    </style>
  </head>
  <body>
    <a href="">Black Link</a>
  </body>
</html>
```

It will produce the following black link –

The :visited pseudo-class

The following is the example which demonstrates how to use the :visited class to set the color of visited links. Possible values could be any color name in any valid format.

```
<html>
  <head>
    <style type="text/css">
      a:visited {color: #006600}
    </style>
  </head>
  <body>
    <a href="">Click this link</a>
  </body>
</html>
```

This will produce following link. Once you will click this link, it will change its color to green.

The :hover pseudo-class

The following example demonstrates how to use the :hover class to change the color of links when we bring a mouse pointer over that link. Possible values could be any color name in any valid format.

```
<html>
  <head>
    <style type="text/css">
      a:hover {color: #FFCC00}
    </style>
```

```html
    </head>
    <body>
      <a href="">Bring Mouse Here</a>
    </body>
</html>
```

It will produce the following link. Now you bring your mouse over this link and you will see that it changes its color to yellow.

The :active pseudo-class

The following example demonstrates how to use the :active class to change the color of active links. Possible values could be any color name in any valid format.

```html
<html>
  <head>
    <style type="text/css">
      a:active {color: #FF00CC}
    </style>
  </head>
  <body>
    <a href="">Click This Link</a>
  </body>
</html>
```

It will produce the following link. When a user clicks it, the color changes to pink.

The :focus pseudo-class

The following example demonstrates how to use the :focus class to change the color of focused links. Possible values could be any color name in any valid format.

```
<html>
  <head>
    <style type="text/css">
      a:focus {color: #0000FF}
    </style>
  </head>
  <body>
    <a href="">Click this Link</a>
  </body>
</html>
```

It will produce the following link. When this link gets focused, its color changes to orange. The color changes back when it loses focus.

The :first-child pseudo-class

The :first-child pseudo-class matches a specified element that is the first child of another element and adds special style to that element that is the first child of some other element.

To make :first-child work in IE <!DOCTYPE> must be declared at the top of document.

For example, to indent the first paragraph of all <div> elements, you could use this definition –

```
<html>
  <head>


    <style type="text/css">
      div > p:first-child
      {
        text-indent: 25px;
      }
    </style>


  </head>
  <body>


    <div>
```

```
    <p>First paragraph in div. This paragraph
will be indented</p>

    <p>Second paragraph in div. This
paragraph will not be indented</p>

    </div>

    <p>But it will not match the paragraph in
this HTML:</p>


<div>

    <h3>Heading</h3>

    <p>The first paragraph inside the div. This
paragraph will not be effected.</p>

    </div>


  </body>
</html>
```

The :lang pseudo-class

The language pseudo-class :lang, allows constructing selectors based on the language setting for specific tags.

This class is useful in documents that must appeal to multiple languages that have different conventions for certain language constructs. For example, the French language typically uses angle brackets (< and >) for quoting purposes, while the English language uses quote marks (' and ').

In a document that needs to address this difference, you can use the :lang pseudo-class to change the quote marks appropriately. The following code changes the <blockquote> tag appropriately for the language being used –

```
<html>
  <head>
    <style type="text/css">
      /* Two levels of quotes for two languages*/
      :lang(en) { quotes: '"' '"' "'" "'"; }
      :lang(fr) { quotes: "<<" ">>" "<" ">"; }
    </style>
  </head>
  <body>
    <p>...<q lang="fr">A quote in a
paragraph</q>...</p>
  </body>
</html>
```

The :lang selectors will apply to all the elements in the document. However, not all elements make use of the quotes property, so the effect will be transparent for most elements.

Pseudo-elements

Pseudo-elements match virtual elements that don't exist explicitly in the document tree. Pseudo-elements can be dynamic, inasmuch as the virtual elements they represent can change, for example, when the width of the browser window is altered. They can also represent content that's generated by CSS rules.

In CSS1 and CSS2, pseudo-elements start with a colon (:), just like pseudo-classes. In CSS3, pseudo-elements start with a double colon (::), which differentiates them from pseudo-classes.

CSS1 gave us :first-letter and :first-line; CSS2 gave us generated content and the :before and :after pseudo-elements; and CSS3 added ::selection.

:first-letter - represents the first character of the first line of text within an element

:first-line- represents the first formatted line of text

:before- specifies content to be inserted before another element

:after- specifies content to be inserted after another element

::selection-represents a part of the document that's been highlighted by the user

:first-letter

The :first-letter pseudo-element is mainly used for creating common typographical effects like drop caps. This pseudo-element represents the first character of the first formatted line of text in a block-level element, an inline block, a table caption, a table cell, or a list item.

No other content (for example, an image) may appear before the text. Certain punctuation characters, like quotation marks, that precede or follow the first character should be included in the pseudo-element. Despite the name, this pseudo-element will also match a digit that happens to be the first character in a block.

If the element is a list item, :first-letter applies to the first character of content after the list item marker unless the property list-style-position is set to inside, in which case the pseudo-element may be ignored by the user agent. If an element includes generated content created with the :before or :after pseudo-elements, :first-letter applies to the content of the element *including* thegenerated content.

The CSS2 specification states that only certain CSS properties are to be supported for this pseudo-class. Let's look at a code fragment that shows how this pseudo-element works:

```
<p>Hello, World!</p>
```

The selector p:first-letter matches the letter H. It's as if there were an extra element in the markup:

```
<p><p:first-letter>H</p:first-letter>ello, World!</p>
```

The above markup isn't valid HTML—it's just a visualization of the pseudo-element concept.

If the first child node of an element is another block element, this pseudo-element will propagate to the child node. Here's an example:

```
<div>
  <p>Hello, World!</p>
</div>
```

Both selectors—div:first-letter and p:first-letter—will match the letter H. The equivalent pseudo-markup is:

```
<div>
  <p>
```

```
<div:first-letter>
  <p:first-letter>H</p:first-letter>
  </div:first-letter>ello, World!
 </p>
</div>
```

:first-line

This pseudo-element represents the first formatted line of text in a block-level element, an inline block, a table caption, or a table cell. As with the :first-letter pseudo-element, the first line may actually occur inside a block-level child element.

The amount of text that's represented by :first-line depends on how the text is rendered—it's affected by factors like font size and line width. If the user changes the text size or the width of the browser window, more or fewer characters could become part of the pseudo-element.

Here's an example rule set and HTML block:

```
p:first-line {
  text-transform: uppercase;
}
```
<p>This is a paragraph of text containing several lines of text.

How this text is broken up into lines by a user agent depends on

how the text is rendered, font properties, size of browser window,

and size of viewing device.</p>

The selector p:first-line will match the first line of text rendered by the user agent. We can see how a user agent might insert the pseudo-element into the HTML block like this:

<p><p:first-line>This is a paragraph of text</p:first-line> containing several lines of text.

How this text is broken up into lines by a user agent depends on how the text is rendered, font

properties, size of browser window, and size of viewing device.</p>

The above markup isn't valid HTML; it's just a visualization of the pseudo-element concept.

If the first child node of an element is another block element, this pseudo-element will propagate to the child node. Here's another example:

<div>

  <p>This is a paragraph of text containing several lines of text. How this text is broken up

into lines by a user agent depends on how the text is rendered, font properties, size of browser

 window, and size of viewing device.</p>

</div>

Both   the div:first-line and p:first-line selectors will be able to be matched in this case. The equivalent pseudo-markup is:

<div>

 <p>

  <div:first-line>

   <p:first-line>This is a paragraph of text</p:first-line>

  </div:first-line> containing several lines of text. How this text is broken up into

   lines by a user agent depends on how the text is rendered, font properties, size of browser

   window, and size of viewing device.</p>

</div>

:before

This   pseudo-element   represents generated content rendered before another element, and is used in conjunction with the content property. Additional properties can be specified to style the pseudo-element. Note that the generated content is only rendered—it doesn't become part of the document tree although the generated content of course will inherit properties from it's parent.

In this example, the text "You are here:" is rendered before the document element with the id value of "breadcrumbs", and given a right margin value of 0.5em:

```
#breadcrumbs:before {
  content: "You are here:";
  margin-right: 0.5em;
}
```

Note: The double colon syntax ::for pseudo-elements is CSS3-only. CSS2.x uses a single colon for both pseudo-elements and pseudo-classes. Therefore support for the single colon version is shown as full in the compatibility table above even if the browser doesn't support the double colon syntax.

:after

This pseudo-element represents generated content that's rendered after another element. This pseudo-element is used in conjunction with the content property, and additional properties can be specified to style it. Note that the generated content is only rendered—it doesn't become part of the document tree although the generated content will of course inherit properties from it's parent.

Example

This example will render the text "cm" in the color #cccccc, after a spanelement with a class value of "centimeters":

```
span.centimeters:after {
  content: "cm";
  color: #cccccc;
}
```

Note: The double colon syntax ::for pseudo-elements is CSS3-only. CSS2.x uses a single colon for both pseudo-elements and pseudo-classes. Therefore support for the single colon version is shown as full in the compatibility table above even if the browser doesn't support the double colon syntax.

::selection

This CSS3 pseudo-element represents a part of the document that's been highlighted by the user, including text in editable text fields. Only a small subset of CSS properties can be used in rules that apply to this pseudo-element; user

agents   must   allow
the background and color properties to be used,
and   can   optionally   allow   the   use   of
the cursor and outline properties.

A selector like textarea::selection will match any
user-selected text within atextarea element.

Chapter 18:
CSS Images

CSS can be used to style images inside HTML pages. By images I mean images included using the img HTML element. In this text will cover the options you have for styling images via the img element with CSS.

margin

The margin CSS property enables you to set the distance between the image and adjacent HTML elements. CSS margins are covered in more detail in my tutorial about margins in CSS.

Actually, the margin is the distance between the border around the image to the adjacent HTML elements. If the image has no border, the margin will be the distance between the edge of the image padding to adjacent HTML elements. If the image has no padding, the margin will be the distance between the image itself to adjacent HTML elements.

border

You can set borders on an image (img element) using the border CSS property. CSS borders are covered in more detail in my tutorial about CSS borders.

Here is an example that sets a border on an image:

```
img.withBorder {
    border: 1px solid #cccccc;
}
```

This example CSS rule sets a 1 pixel gray border around all img elements which have the CSS classwithBorder (<img class="withBorder">)

padding

The padding CSS property sets the distance between the image and its border. Padding is covered in more detail in my tutorial about padding in CSS.

Here is an example that sets both padding and border around an image:

```
img.withBorderAndPadding {
    padding : 10px;
    border  : 1px solid #cccccc;
}
```

width and height

You can use the width and height CSS properties to set the width and height of an image. The width andheight CSS properties are also covered in my tutorial about the CSS box model.

If you set a width and height that is different from the image's own width and height, then the browser will scale the image up or down to match the width and height you set. Here are some width and height CSS examples:

```
img.scaledUp {
    width: 300px;
    height: 150px;
}
img.scaledDown {
    width: 300px;
    height: 150px;
}
```

Scaling images by setting both width and height may result in distorted images, meaning the aspect ratio between width and height might be lost. To scale an image while preserving aspect ratio, set only the width orheight CSS property. The browser will then calculate the other aspect (height, if width is set, or width, if height is set) based on the set width or height, so the aspect ratio of the image is kept. Here are two examples which set only the width and height:

```
img.scaledUp {
    width: 300px;
}
img.scaledDown {
    height: 150px;
}
```

Keeping Image Aspect Ratio

Scaling images by setting both width and height may result in distorted images, meaning the aspect ratio between width and height might be lost. To scale an image while preserving aspect ratio, set only the width orheight CSS property. The browser will then calculate the other aspect (height, if width is set, or width, if height is set) based on the set width or height, so the aspect ratio of the image is kept. Here are two examples which set only the width and height:

```
img.scaledUp {
    width: 300px;
}
img.scaledDown {
    height: 150px;
}
```

Width and Height as Percentages

You can set width and height to percentages. In that case the image will get a width and / or height which is a percentage of the width or height of its parent HTML element. Here is an example:

```
img.percentages {
    width: 25%;
}
```

This examples sets the width of the image to 25% of its parent HTML element width. If the parent HTML element is scaled up or down in size, so is the image.

max-width and max-height

You can set a maximum width and height for the image using the max-width and max-height CSS properties.

Setting a maximum width or height can be useful if the image is using percentages as width or height. In case the user maximizes the browser, perhaps you don't want your image to be scaled up to fill the full browser window (or whatever size the image's parent element has). Setting a maximum width and height might be useful in that case. Here is an example setting a max-width on an image:

```
img.withMaxWidth {
    width: 100%;
    max-width: 500px;
}
```

This example CSS rule sets the width of the img element with the CSS class withMaxWidth to 100% of its parent element. However, the example limits the image to a maximum width of 500px. Once the image reaches a width of 500 pixels, the browser will no longer scale it up, regardless of the width of the parent element.

min-width and min-height

The min-width and min-height CSS properties work like the max-width and max-height CSS properties, except the set a minimum width and height for the image (or whatever HTML element they are applied to.

Responsive Images

Responsive images are images that are part of a responsive web design and which behave accordingly. A responsive web design is a web design which is capable of responding sensibly to the device it is being viewed on, whether that device be a mobile phone, tablet, laptop, desktop or TV.

On a small screen you might want to show smaller images than on a large screen. You might also want to limit the size of an image to fit inside smaller screens (using max-width).

Image Opacity

Creating transparent images with CSS is easy. The CSS opacity property is a part of the CSS3 recommendation.

First we will show you how to create a transparent image with CSS.

Regular image:

```
<!DOCTYPE html>
<html>
<head>
<style>
img {
    opacity: 0.4;
    filter: alpha(opacity=40); /* For IE8 and earlier */
}
</style>
</head>
<body>
<h1>Image Transparency</h1>
<img src="klematis.jpg" width="150" height="113" alt="klematis">
</body>
```

The opacity property can take a value from 0.0 - 1.0. The lower value, the more transparent.

IE8 and earlier use filter:alpha(opacity=x). The x can take a value from 0 - 100. A lower value makes the element more transparent.

Hover Effect

```
<!DOCTYPE html>
<html>
<head>
<style>
img {
    opacity: 0.4;
    filter: alpha(opacity=40); /* For IE8 and earlier */
}

img:hover {
    opacity: 1.0;
    filter: alpha(opacity=100); /* For IE8 and earlier */
}
</style>
</head>
<body>
<h1>Image Transparency</h1>
<img src="klematis.jpg" width="150" height="113" alt="klematis">
<img src="klematis2.jpg" width="150" height="113" alt="klematis">
```

We have added what should happen when a user hovers over one of the images. In this case we want the image to NOT be transparent when the user hovers over it. The CSS for this is opacity:1;.

When the mouse pointer moves away from the image, the image will be transparent again.

www.ingramcontent.com/pod-product-compliance
Lightning Source LLC
Chambersburg PA
CBHW071417050326
40689CB00010B/1873